WAY
TO
BE

FORTY INSIGHTS AND
TRANSFORMATIVE PRACTICES IN THE
HEART OF BEING

TEJPAL
& SHARI GOOTTER

ACKNOWLEDGEMENTS: ON BEING ACKNOWLEDGED

This is a unique book that will help many people. Drawing on their substantial experience and wisdom, the authors guide readers to self-discovery and awareness, offering novel insights and strategies that will allow them to find their own "Way to Be."

- **Andrew Weil, MD, author of *8 Weeks to Optimum Health and Spontaneous Happiness***

Being rather than doing? There are already thousands of books about this topic on Amazon. And those books you bought and never finished because there was no place to dig in your toes and find enough traction to change anything about your doing life. This book is different.

If taken to heart, these 40 "Be" practices offer a profound taste of how to live in your body, kinder and more awake. Don't miss this opportunity.

- **Deborah Jones, Spiritual Director Nine Gates Mystery School**

It takes 40 days to develop a new habit, but only one to change your life—the day you buy Way to Be. Wise, witty, and insightful, this transformational book has 40 practical chapters that don't just teach you how to be mindful—but how to "Be Kind"… "Be Playful"… "Be Sacred," and "Be Wrong"—just to name a few. This is the perfect gift for yourself or someone else you truly love. Open any chapter and find a new…Way to Be.

- **Keith Merryman & David A. Newman, Screen- writers of *Friends with Benefits and Think Like a Man*.**

ON BEING THANKFUL

We are grateful for the enthusiasm and support of many throughout this project. We would especially like to thank:

Paulette and Joe Gootter for their ideas and dedication to making this project successful.

Alex Gootter for his unique insights and assistance.

Claudine Messing for sharing her voice for the audio version of our book.

Leslie Lee, for warmly welcoming us into her magical country house, where we finalized our first draft.

Kristin Davis, our editor, for her kind spirit and her ability to work with us without imposing her point of view.

The whole team at Franklin Rose Publishing, especially Alyson Gannon, for their passion, dedication, and clarity in publishing and promoting our book.

CONTENTS

INTRODUCTION

ON BEING GRATEFUL

Thank you! We are so grateful for your interest in this book. We acknowledge and appreciate your curiosity and openness, knowing the path of being is not always a fairy tale. As we dive into being instead of doing, we create harmony within ourselves and others. As we dive into being instead of doing, we embrace the impermanence and fragility of our existence. As we dive into being instead of doing, we allow our diversity to come together, creating a tapestry that is a gift to the world. Being is not about "be-having;" don't attach yourself to being one way or another. Have fun with it.

ON BEING TRANSFORMED

The journey of personal transformation is not about reaching happiness, or any peaks; it is about going inward so we can see what is beyond our fears, our rejections, and our judgements.

As you go within, you may encounter unintended pain and discomfort. When we are able to be with our agitated mind, without grabbing for a better future or running away from a difficult situation, we are able to open our heart. An open heart brings lucidity, compassion, and detachment. When this happens, we can step away from any emotional waves of life, whether we call them great or awful.

Practice, patience, and repetition are the necessary ingredients to create healing and inner clarity. From there we develop a neutral mind; the pathway to peace regardless of what shows up in our lives.

ON BEING US

Tejpal 's Journey

Let's face it; I've come a long way. I am now able to play and dance with life, but it did not start this way.

I was born in France and for as long as I can remember I was extremely unhappy. I felt disconnected and, in a way, nauseated to be alive. At a very early age I contemplated death, as I could not find any meaning and connection in this world and my life.

I survived my late teens by reading French litera-
ture from the 20th century, listening to classical
music, often skipping school, and smoking pot. I
had no idea who I was and was terrified to become
an adult.

Without a sense of clear purpose, I went to univer-
sity and chose to study psychology knowing that it
would be beneficial regardless of my future work.
Once I got my masters degree, still unsure about
what to do with my life, I decided to get an MBA
and eventually got my first job.

Work became a revelation: I felt recognized and
appreciated. Very quickly I took on some important leadership roles and realized that despite my
passion, my creativity, my vision, and my hard
work, I did not have the right relationship skills. I
was too impulsive, too judgmental, and too emotional. I also had too much fear and too much ego
to ask for help.

At the age of thirty-three I decided to leave my
good paying job, my country, and the relationship
I was in. I moved from Paris to NYC in December

1994. I was full of fear, yet I knew I would not turn around. Upon my arrival in the US, I stayed for two weeks in an ashram in up-state New York. I hoped my fears would go away, but they did not. With the help of a great therapist, I learned to feel my experience without shame and embrace who I was.

Through my journey I met great teachers and healers and wonderful friends who helped me in my transformation; at the time, they felt like angels who carried me.

During the years, always searching and seeking deeper healing and greater insights, I went back to various schools to become an energy healer, a life coach and a kundalini yoga instructor. Today I combine all my skills to offer one on one sessions, weekly classes on yoga, intuition, soul mission and vibrant living, as well as workshops in the field of spirituality.

Never ever could I have imagined the transformation I would go through and the healing that took place within me that would create a deep sense of peace and joy in my life. I now know it is a never-ending journey of ups and downs and everything becomes a learning opportunity.

Meeting Shari

Shari came to my Monday night Kundalini Yoga with her guide dog, Indy. Her presence touched me deeply. There is a depth that holds no words, and in a way that is not romantic, I fell in love with Shari: we became sisters. Her quick ability to comprehend everything, her great sense of humor, and her compassion were simply priceless. Within less than a year we decided to co-create together, teach together, and write this book. I am forever grateful for this sacred friendship.

Shari's Journey

It should be easy to tell my story, after all I am a therapist.

Although I don't remember my early years, I know they were filled with physical challenges and pain. I was diagnosed with juvenile rheumatoid arthritis at the age of two. When I was six years old, my family moved from New York to Arizona for my well-being. I am extremely lucky to have great parents who took care of me and taught me unconditional love.

The arthritis went into remission, and I had a very fortunate upbringing, never knowing that we moved because of my condition. My college time was full of travels, learning, and great adventures. I met wonderful people who are still my best friends today.

My sense of adventure led me to Brazil. I lived there for about seven years. That time was filled with rich culture, discoveries, and personal and professional growth. My entrepreneurial spirit woke up. From night clubs to clothing design, I was on a roll: nothing was out of reach. During this time, I became a mom, which was the most life-affirming experience.

Returning to Tucson, my vision was decreasing. Although I was losing my sight, I was not losing my way. Through the love and support of my family and friends, I went through more physical and personal challenges, including surgeries and divorce. I also experienced the sudden loss of my brother.

This tragedy and grief brought family and friends together to create a foundation in his memory.

I turned challenges and potential barriers into life lessons and dreams. I did numerous trainings and became a yoga teacher. I finished my master's degree and became a therapist.

I did a lot of volunteer work and eventually led a nationally recognized program for high school students. I created and facilitated workshops in the field of leadership, diversity, and personal growth for youth, adults, and therapists.

Today my life is filled with love and gratitude. I have been blessed with a true-life partner. The breadth and depth of my work brings me joy and purpose. I love and nurture my family, my friends, and my animals. These relationships greatly support and encourage me and are the key to my essence.

MEETING TEJPAL

It was meant to be, and I still wonder why it took so long. What I feel in this relationship has no limit. I wonder if I will ever be able to describe what we share. We have similar interests and paths and had attended many of the same workshops before we finally met. When we are together, whether it is writing, traveling, or working, it is timeless. There is magic.

ON BEING THE READER

We have chosen forty ways to be, for you to explore. In the yogic tradition, it takes forty days to create a new habit. Therefore, it takes forty days to start a process of personal transformation. Each practice is presented through specific lenses in a concise manner. Some titles may surprise and attract you, yet look at each one, as the content may not be what you expect.

There is no specific order of the practices, and you can dive in any way you wish. The following are a couple of suggestions:

- You can do one practice a day and go through the whole book.
- You can do the same practice for forty days.
- You can open the book randomly and make that page the practice of the day.

- You can choose the practices which attract you the most, doing them until you feel inspired to choose another.
- You can pick a practice a week and share your process with someone or a group.
- The options are endless, and they are all good.

As in any kind of practice, consistency is where magic happens.

ON BEING CONSISTENT

Who wants to be consistent? We need adventure, change, and diversity, right? Being consistent seems as though you will fall asleep from boredom. Change, new, and different are very appealing.

But what happens when you are not consistent?

- You don't get results.
- You don't go deep.
- Your mind experiences agitation.
- You fall into old patterns.
- You don't create transformation.
- You stay stuck.

Consistency is the core of any practice. It allows us to integrate our learning and doing into being.

BE AGELESS

Being ageless is not about anti-aging or staying young. It is about accepting who we are on earth, without identifying ourselves through the lenses of age. Playfulness does not stop at eight years old. Silliness does not stop at three years old, passion does not stop at twenty-five years old and learning never stops.

As we take our first breath when we are born, the clock begins ticking, and we don't know when our time of physical death will occur. We all age, and as we do our physical and spiritual selves change. We are also diminishing and shrinking. Our physical stature becomes smaller; our strength weakens, and sometimes our minds grow cloudy.

Aging is accepted differently depending on our traditions and culture. In the United States, after the age of thirty-five, many people want to look younger; the anti-aging market is a booming business. Americans tend to have strong negative feelings regarding aging.

In Africa, because they hold wisdom, the elders are the ones who are truly respected, and thus the first to be consulted when conflicts occur. They live with their families, being cared for and honored as their time of death nears.

As in Africa, Indian and Asian cultures honor their elders. The family stays connected; old and young living together and learning to be, with the diversity of rhythms, abilities, experiences, knowledge, and wisdom. These cultures don't fight or resist the idea of aging or dying, as we do in America. In the United States, elders are frequently placed together in special communities. Sadly, they are often then forgotten.

Being ageless is not about pretending time does not exist or that we don't get older or that we never die. It is not about fighting the process of aging. It is an attitude of "being in the moment" with who we are, our beauty, and our limitations of the day.

Being ageless is about embracing our mortality and practicing curiosity regarding our aging process. Rather than denying what is, we invite it in and learn to dance and laugh with it. If death becomes part of our identity, then our life carries fewer struggles. We still can have deep sorrow and despair regarding the loss of a loved one, yet, we remember our true nature.

As soon as you accept aging, you truly become ageless, because, at that moment, you are not limiting yourself to one aspect of your experience. Instead, you are preparing and training yourself for the transition of dying, perhaps *la crème de la crème* as far as letting go is concerned.

Suzanne, one of Shari's dearest friends, is in her eighties and has practiced yoga for over five decades. Over the years, she has adapted and changed her practice. When she attends classes, due to her age, she uses props and modifies many poses. Yet, she is still able to enjoy yoga and always feels more relaxed after class. Suzanne has accepted that aging requires some changes and modifications, yet, she also knows that aging does not mean she must give up the things she is passionate about. She has embraced "being ageless."

As our physical body slows down, our role is to accept the changes and to be willing to engage and connect with ourselves and others differently. Holding on to what we were able to accomplish in the past creates suffering and disconnection. When we embrace aging, we embrace the law of life, which is constant change. Each of us will age differently. Some of us will lose our hearing, our sight, our flexibility, or our memory. There is a true unknown as to how our body evolves. Our role is to welcome aging with grace.

When we choose to be ageless, we remember that we are more than our physical bodies. Many spiritual traditions have described human beings as a combination of several bodies.

In the Kabbalah tradition, we have nine bodies; in Kundalini yoga tradition, we have ten bodies; and in the ancient Egyptian tradition, we have nine bodies (different than the Kabbalah tradition). In brief, no matter which spiritual tradition we are talking about, the physical is only one dimension of who we are. Yet, death is still taboo in American society, and rarely do we allow ourselves to have a conversation about death with an elder.

Every time we are not attaching to what ages within us and around us, every time we are not holding on, our life has an opportunity to flow and our spirit to glow.

THE PRACTICE

MEDITATION: LETTING GO

This breathing technique focuses on holding the breath out after the exhale, which helps the mind to slow down, relax, and let go. If you are not familiar with this practice, it may feel uncomfortable at first. The repetition of this technique will help the quality of your relaxation.

- Sit in a comfortable position. Lengthen your spine and draw your shoulders down your back. Soften your face and your jaw. Close your eyes.
- Tune in and notice your breath: is it fast or slow, deep or shallow? Is it smooth or scattered? Notice how your body feels.

Where do you feel a flow, and where do you feel constricted? What parts of your body feel vibrant?

Start the following breath pattern:

- Breathe in through the nose for a count of four.
- Breathe out through the nose for a count of four.
- Pause at the bottom of the exhale for a minimum of four counts. The goal is to hold the breath out and find your edge.
- Continue for five minutes.

JOURNALING

- What are your fears about aging?
- If you knew you only had twenty-four hours to live, how would you spend your time?

TAKE ACTION

- Participate in an activity that is multi-generational. For example: Attend a spiritual service, a fundraising walk for an organization, etc.

BE CAREFUL

"*Be careful!*" Can you hear the worries embedded in this statement? "*Be careful!*" Can you feel the fear in your body, perhaps in your lungs, your shoulders, or your stomach? "*Be careful!*" Can you hear what is not said? "*Please be safe, I don't want something bad happening to you, and I don't want to lose you.*"

What if instead of focusing on possible dangers, being careful meant being full of care for oneself? What if you considered yourself precious enough to really listen to your needs and make the appropriate changes in your lifestyle and relationships? What if every day you chose to wake up with a spirit of devotion and service toward yourself? By doing so, do you believe you are becoming complacent or selfish?

The more you listen to your state of being, the more centered you are. The more you pay attention to what is going on within you, the less reactive and emotional you become. The more you embrace your full self, the more authentic you are and the better you connect to the rest of the world.

Paying attention to you does not mean indulging. It means, like an athlete in training, you know your limitations, therefore you don't get injured. It means you know what lifts you up, so that your spirit stays high. It means you know what motivates you, so you can keep going despite any kind of adversity. In this context, self-care is not ego-driven, but service driven.

Now, let's go a step further. To fully care about yourself, you will need to go deep into the unprocessed and unresolved parts of who you are. These are the parts of you that have been buried deep in your unconscious mind and may carry shame, jealousy, or rejection, to name a few. Being "care full" is about caring for your shadow; it is about embracing all of who you are. It is about welcoming the wounded, distorted aspects of you, not from a place of pity or victimhood, but from a place of compassion and clarity.

The journey is not always a walk in the park. As you commit to meet your true self over and over again, look for ways to nurture you. When you engage in this process, you realize that being careful is not about me versus you. It is about developing the healer within: patient, present, neutral, and clear.

THE PRACTICE

MEDITATION: CHECKING IN

This meditation helps train the mind to focus on your sensations and experiences, thus supporting you to stay present. The more you stay connected to your physical body, the less your mind wanders.

- Lie down and start a body scan. A body scan is a way to bring mindful awareness as you notice any physical sensations in the different parts of your body.
- We recommend closing your eyes, noticing and observing.
- Scan your body starting at your feet, moving up to the ankles and calves, then to the legs and knees. Keep moving up, slowly, to the top of your head.
- Pause at each part, tighten and relax.

- Notice your sensations and emotions.
- Do you feel hot or cold, tense or relaxed? Are you tired or energized? Are you agitated or peaceful? Are there parts of your body that require attention?
- Once you have done your self-assessment, keep your eyes closed and stay curious. What do you need today: more support, more time alone, more playtime, more clearing time, etc.?

JOURNALING

- Are there any physical parts of you that you keep rejecting?
- Are there any of your behaviors that bring shame?
- What do you need to change in your lifestyle to enhance your self-care?

TAKE ACTION

- As we want you to accept yourself fully, share with a loved one (it can be a friend, a family member, a life partner, etc.) a part of you that you find troublesome. It can be irrational fears, shame, or guilt, or any part of you that you know is misaligned.

BE CLUELESS

There is no curriculum for developing the ability to be clueless. To our knowledge, there are no Ph.D. dissertations on this topic either. Most often, cluelessness is confused with being dumb or stupid, when in actuality, it refers to a state of being completely unaware, bewildered, or confused. We suggest you take a different look at being clueless. For example, think of being clueless not as being stupid or dumb, but as being open to learning and willing to explore.

The mind refuses to be clueless. It loves to label, categorize, make assumptions, and come to conclusions. The mind thinks it knows everything and likes to boss us around. The mind loves to move forward, yet being clueless is about stepping back and pausing.

The problem is that we often listen to the mind and let it run the show. When the mind is in control, it compares, analyzes, or worries. The mind is a troublemaker, in the sense that it tends to over-analyze and overthink.

The mind also needs to think in a nonlinear way. Teach your mind to think in 360 degrees; teach your mind to let your bones, blood, and cells think. Instead of trying to understand what is going on, shift your focus and experience what is happening at that exact moment. Instead of listening only to the content of a conversation, allow yourself to listen to your inner experience. Pay attention to all your senses.

Being clueless also involves being open and receptive, and not pushing and obsessing to find a solution. The mind loves to be a detective and creates meaning for everything. It gives the illusion that it is in control, on top of everything, and responsible for every situation.

The biggest challenge in this practice is truly allowing yourself to be in an unknown space first. Let the mind spin if it wants to, but don't follow the thoughts your mind produces. If you skip this phase, your mind will create its own story, as it does not like pausing or being still.

At one of our workshops, participants were asked to work in pairs and to hold an object belonging to another person. The purpose of the exercise was to tune in to the energy of the object and observe the experience throughout the body. Jillian was holding what seemed to be a wedding ring. She began to create a story. During Jillian's sharing it was clear that she did not allow herself to step back, pause, and feel. She thought she knew.

Being clueless becomes more challenging when you face a crisis, but that may be when you need this skill the most. The more the mind wants to jump in, the more confused you will be. Slow down and drop into your physical, emotional, and spiritual self instead of racing to look for an answer, speeding up and spinning out of control, or being consumed. Choose to engage the non-mental parts of you when you face a challenge.

There is a childlike quality to being clueless, and a sense of adventure. When you are not attached to knowing what is next, there is freedom and playfulness. Answers come when you don't look for them. The more clueless you are, the more insights you gain.

THE PRACTICE

MEDITATION: GUIDED MEDITATION

This guided meditation will open and enhance your senses and bring relaxation to encourage the practice of being clueless.

- Find a quiet place and choose whether to sit, stand, or lie down.
- Close your eyes.
- Imagine yourself in a forest. Listen to the birds and the wind, smell the pine trees and the flowers, feel the sun and crisp air on your skin, let your body bask in the beauty of your surroundings. As you breathe in, notice your senses. What do you hear, smell, or feel? As you exhale, let everything go.
- Continue for three minutes.

JOURNALING

- Find a quiet place, come to standing and take a moment to ground.

- Soften your gaze.
- Choose a situation you have been thinking about and want to gain more clarity. Notice your state of mind; breathe and take a step back.
- Pause and call on the witness within; be aware of your sensations.
- Turn 90 degrees to the right and pause. Take a couple of breaths and notice your sensations.
- Turn 90 degrees to the right and pause. Take a couple of breaths and notice your sensations.
- Turn 90 degrees to the right again and pause. Take a couple of breaths and notice your sensations.
- Pause and return to your breath. What did you notice? How did you see the situation differently? Journal about your insights.

TAKE ACTION

- Before a conversation, an interaction, or a meeting, pause and acknowledge your preconceived ideas and the potential consequences that you are creating. If the situation allows, share the story you are making up; this may help you stay open and present. Otherwise, take note of the story.

BE CONCISE

What would happen if you decided to think and speak concisely for one day? The beauty of conciseness is that you must choose your words carefully. You need to pause and think before you open your mouth. You need to select wisely what and how you want to communicate.

We are not concise because we are rushing to the next thing; when one is concise, it is because one cares. At times it may appear you are being concise, but you are most likely shutting down. Conciseness is not about hiding, holding your thoughts, and sharing very little. It is about wisely expressing yourself with simplicity and clarity. If you want to be understood, you need to be concise. For example, while driving or putting together furniture, concise and simple directions are easier to follow.

If you want to solve problems, you need to consistently be concise. Being concise invites you to focus on what is important. At times, you might find it difficult to be concise because your agenda is to convince. Other times you might find it difficult to be concise because you are afraid of the possible reactions. Despite this, these challenges present growth opportunities.

It takes courage to be concise, direct, and forthcoming. It may be easier to dilute, diffuse, and hide behind an excess of words and explanations. Being concise teaches you to hone in on the essence; it takes focus. It also presents risks, as the recipients have time and space to respond.

The ego often struggles with being concise. Ego has a lot to say and share and loves to be the center of attention.

When you choose to be concise, you choose authenticity and transparency; you are not trying to impress, seduce, or manipulate; you stay neutral.

Since social media and texting are so prevalent in our society, we are often concise. But this type of conciseness does not assist us in learning the art of being concise. Too often, this invites reactivity, loud opinions, and not necessarily thoughtful expressions. The type of conciseness we want you to strive for is meaningful, well thought out and offers true connection with others, as opposed to just "tweeting" at one another. A concise sentence with a genuine connection can convey much more than any tweet or social media post, regardless of how long.

If you approach conciseness in a mindful way, if you are thoughtful and heart-centered in your communication, you will go deeper in your self-awareness and expression, and away from possible drama. There is no need to be blunt, you can still be compassionate and to the point.

Relate to conciseness as an art form; center yourself, slow down, and connect to the essence of what you want to share. In other words, be a minimalist.

THE PRACTICE

MEDITATION: "CLEAR UP/CALM DOWN"

This simple breathing technique incorporates a short mantra inviting you to stay vibrant as the body relaxes.

- Sit in a comfortable position. Lengthen your spine and draw your shoulders down your back. Soften your face and your jaw. Close your eyes.
- As you inhale from the base of your spine up to the crown of your head, mentally repeat, "Clear Up."
- As you exhale from the crown of your head all the way down to the base of your spine, mentally repeat, "Calm down."
- Continue for three minutes.

JOURNALING

- Think of a time it was difficult to be concise and journal about what was in the way.

TAKE ACTION

- Before you interact, speak, or text, pause, gather your thoughts and decide the message you really want to convey. Narrow your intention to three key words.
- Choose one situation and practice daily for a week. An example: Interactions with a co-worker or family member or written communication.

BE CONNECTED

As human beings, we have an inherent need to connect; it is part of every dimension of our lives. Connection has the ability to heal us, destroy us, open us, and teach us, depending on our mindset and behavior. Knowing when and how to connect is vital in navigating life. Connecting with others allows us to live fully and meaningfully.

In the world we live in unplugging often seems like the thing to do, as we can easily be over-whelmed with any number of threats, crises, and catastrophes. Staying away from the news and the noise is tempting, and at times necessary. Yet, being connected and aware of what is happening on this planet is our human responsibility. We need to learn to be with the chaos and crises without drifting away. We need to stay rooted and not sink into despair, while also learning to stand up or sit still in the middle of the storm. Our role is to stay open to learning and healing.

If a hurricane destroys part of a country, feel it; if a culture is being threatened and bombed, feel it; if injustice happens, feel it. Don't fall into the drama, and do keep your light on. Even in tragedy, we can still be connected without being overwhelmed or losing ourselves.

Deborah owns a local restaurant in Shari's neighborhood. The spouse of one of Deborah's employees was recently diagnosed with cancer. Deborah decided to have an evening where all proceeds would go to this employee's family. Everyone involved that evening felt closer, had an opportunity to open their hearts and show their support. Thus, Deborah and all the employees felt closer and connected through this one event.

When we look at interpersonal relationships, our role is to stay open to possibilities and express our vulnerability. As we connect, new strengths, new visions, new skills, and new energies emerge. This may not always be comfortable to do, and we may find that sometimes others are a source of suffering. Through relationships, we have the opportunity to speak up, serve, ask, listen, and open up so that we become more aware of our strengths and limitations. A relationship is a mirror which provides us with an opportunity to self-reflect and gain new understanding of who we are.

Being part of a community can be challenging, as we may not be like-minded, although we may have a shared goal or purpose, thus allowing for growth and development.

True connections are constantly changing; they give us the ability to shift, and they widen our horizons. If our connections hold the same pattern, if we fall into the same routine and/or the same roles in our relationships, we are simply falling asleep.

Connection to others requires the ability to connect to oneself. For this, we need to enjoy time alone to rest and rejuvenate. Acknowledging and respecting our needs, communicating, and setting boundaries are essential for authentic relationships.

Decide how much information about this world you are able to digest without being lost, depressed, or agitated. Stay present; reach out to others. Choose the pace and shape of your relationships in order to feel nourished and enhanced.

THE PRACTICE

MEDITATION: CONNECTION TO SELF

Changing breath patterns broadens your experience and allows for deeper understanding and connection to self.

- Sit in a comfortable position. Lengthen your spine and draw your shoulders down your back. Soften your face and your jaw. Close your eyes.
- Inhale quickly and exhale slowly through the nose, repeat this cycle for two minutes.
- Inhale slowly and exhale quickly through the nose, repeat this cycle for two minutes.
- Relax and return to your natural rhythm.
- Did you feel a difference between these two breath patterns?

JOURNALING

- Choose a connection and write about what makes it special. Example: Write about your connection with nature, music, culture, a person, an animal, a teacher, etc.

TAKE ACTION

- Think of a person you want to connect to; it could be someone you may or may not already be connected to.
- What would you need to do to create authentic connection?
- Write down your guidelines for authentic connection.
- Now, reach out to this person.

BE COOL

Everyone wants to have the right look, the right social media platform, or the right hobby, especially when we are young and still discovering who we are. When we have the "right" things, we feel cool. We all know that if you are cool, you are in. If you were a hippie from the sixties, being cool meant you were laid-back, you didn't sweat the small stuff, and you took it easy. Today, if you don't fall into one of these two categories, what are we talking about? We are referring to your ability to stay peaceful and still inside, no matter what.

If we listen to the yogis, we are made of five gross elements: earth, water, fire, air, and ether. Each of these elements plays a role in our system and has its own unique set of qualities. The balance of these five elements supports our health and happiness. In order to stay "cool," particular attention must be given to the fire element. This is because the energy of fire is necessary to digest and process food. It also allows anger to be expressed and feeds our courage and passion. It helps us to be focused and resilient, yet, too much fire in our life is all-encompassing. Everything becomes a source of irritation, anger, or anxiety.

If you live mainly on the energy of fire, you may have a lot of energy, but you consume a lot as well. Chances are, you end up being at the center of everything which does not serve you or the people around you; your impatience and reactivity are too loud. When your fire within is taking over, you have a strong sense of self and can be too aggressive in your assessment and at times dismissive of other points of view. This level of reactivity can also be a defense mechanism as fiery people don't like to show their vulnerability and insecurity.

Sergio recently attended one of our workshops. Participants were asked to do some introspective work, then share and listen to each other's. Sergio's fire prevented him from listening to the instructions and being present. When he shared, it was overbearing, and he was unaware of how it impacted others.

Inflammation is the source of many diseases. Anti-inflammatory diets have been well researched and promoted to support health. Why not focus on an anti-inflammatory lifestyle and mindset? If you constantly arrive late to appointments, if you always eat on the go, if the volume on your radio or television is loud, or if you rush into things, chances are you will be agitated, and your system will be negatively impacted.

Practicing being cool is choosing not to use yelling and screaming as a communication style; it is choosing to step back instead of jumping in. It is being considerate of the impact of your words, thoughts, and actions towards others.

Being cool is not pretending everything is great. There is no need to wear a mask or use the emoji with sunglasses; we want you to be true to yourself and still feel a wide range of emotions.

To do this, first, pay attention to your mind. Notice if your mind keeps repeating the same thought and can't let it go. Secondly, feel your feelings, change your narrative, and practice mindfulness.

Allow yourself to experience your senses in a non-judgmental way. Following these steps will inevitably "cool" things down.

After intense physical activity, cooling down helps you to relax and recover faster. The same applies in life; if you get caught in heated situations, remember to cool down and move on.

THE PRACTICE

MEDITATION: COOLING BREATH

This technique helps you to release extra fire and develop your sensitivity.

- Sit in a comfortable position. Lengthen your spine and draw your shoulders down your back. Soften your face and your jaw. Close your eyes.
- Open your mouth, stick your tongue out, and roll your tongue.
- Inhale through your rolled tongue.
- Close your mouth and exhale through your nose.
- Continue for three minutes minimum.

JOURNALING

- Recall a moment where you were triggered and became fiery. Make a list of things that have been, or could be, helpful to calm down.

TAKE ACTION

- For one day, notice your reactivity. In the situations where you are escalating, practice calming techniques and make changes to your lifestyle.

BE DETACHED

We live in a world where we become attached to a lot of things. We are attached to our health, our life before we die, another person when in love, objects that we own, our lifestyle, our status, the image of who we think we are, and the list goes on. We are constantly drawn to and tempted to create attachments at many levels.

Detachment means accepting what exists at any given moment. It is not that we don't care or choose to ignore something or are insensitive. It means despite the wide range of emotions we may have vis-à-vis of a person or a situation, we decide to step back instead of jumping in and reacting.

There is a fine line between attachment and desire. When attachment to health takes over, we slow the healing process. When there is a desire to be healthy, we trust the body will heal, and that life will unfold the way it is supposed to.

When we become attached at the physical level, aging becomes a challenge. There is a constant obsession with how we look and what our bodies can do and cannot do. We let our mind and ego win and we may become narcissistic. Our image is "everything" and we believe it is the foundation for our happiness. Chasing youth at the physical level separates you from your true self and shuts your heart down.

When we become attached in loving relationships, there is usually tremendous pain and fear that goes with the attachment. It seems impossible to separate from one another, there is also an inability to embrace each other. Little by little, depending on your personality and the relational dynamic, routine or drama takes over.

When we become attached at the mental level, opinion seems the way to think and being right and wrong become central to any discussion. The ability to be curious, ask, question, and stay open is gone.

When we believe our attachments must be manifested, we experience constant suffering, constant blaming, and perhaps addictive patterns. Our role is to dive into our attachments, feel our void, and discover the needs that have not been met.

When we sense ourselves becoming rigid, as to how our life should be, we know there is attachment, and we need to look at what we are desperately holding onto.

Embrace *detachment,* and your life will flow. It will enhance your playfulness and creative self- expression.

THE PRACTICE

MEDITATION: RESET THE MIND

This meditation helps you to balance the right and left hemispheres of the brain and strengthens your nervous system.

- Sit in a comfortable position. Lengthen your spine and draw your shoulders down your back. Soften your face and your jaw. Close your eyes.
- Block the right nostril with your right thumb, inhale through the left nostril and pause, mentally vibrate the mantra SA TA NA MA.

- Release your right thumb and block the left nostril with your right index finger, exhale through the right nostril and pause, mentally vibrate the mantra SA TA NA MA.
- Inhale through the right nostril and pause, mentally vibrate the mantra SA TA NA MA.
- Release your right index finger and block the right nostril with your right thumb, exhale through the left nostril and pause, mentally vibrate the mantra SA TA NA MA.
- Repeat this sequence for three minutes.
- Vibrating the mantra SA TA NA MA invites you to let go. (The translation of the mantra is: Infinity, Life, Death, Rebirth.)

JOURNALING

- Choose something or someone you are attached to. Write about the benefits and drawbacks.

TAKE ACTION

- Every day, for a minimum of fourteen days, choose an object or possession to give away or get rid of.

BE DISCIPLINED

Discipline is not about going to the gym every day, eating healthy, and keeping a strict schedule. It is not about accomplishing extreme challenges. It *is* about one aspect of your life that needs to be revisited: self-care. Self-care requires balance; it takes more discipline to create moderation.

You may think that if you are disciplined, nothing gets in the way. You can face any adversity no matter what the challenges are; you have enough will and motivation to get things done.

If discipline is outcome driven, you will never be at peace or content. You will always run after the next challenge, and often the results you are chasing are chasing you. The danger is in creating so much rigidity that the only way you can relate to yourself is through your accomplishments. When this happens, you will most likely develop a high level of alertness, some form of anxiety, and the inability to rest. You are then trapped in this cycle and feel lost. At this point, you have lost the ability to be discerning and true to self.

The purpose of discipline is to go beyond polarities. If you only follow your emotions, you will go through highs and lows, excitement and depression, addiction and reaction, seduction and rejection. You will not be able to access the wisdom of the heart and its stability. Emotions are the spice of life, they are beautiful when they enhance our experience, but not when they overpower. If every action you take is emotionally driven, everything becomes impulsive and reactive. Chances are you will live in constant drama. The beauty of discipline is that it teaches us to put our emotions at bay. We commit to something not for short term rewards, but long-term benefits; we know that we will gain peace after all.

When you go beyond the intensity of your emotions, you are free. The discipline is being able to stay in the middle. It may not seem exciting, and you may believe your energy or passion will diminish. In fact, the opposite is true. In the neutrality of self-care, in this quiet place that is not lead by the ego, you may connect to an infinite amount of creative energy, but, if you keep the intensity too high, you can't hear what is truly going on.

When you realize the purpose of discipline is inner transformation and not achievement, your discipline is no longer a chore, and you no longer identify yourself by your successes or failures. Discipline *is* the path to happiness.

THE PRACTICE

MEDITATION: BALANCING BREATH

This breathing technique helps reduce anxiety and cravings. It may also support the quality of your sleep. By reducing your reactivity and agitation, you will be able to create a level of consistency in your lifestyle and practice the discipline of staying neutral.

- Sit in a comfortable position. Lengthen your spine and draw your shoulders down your back. Soften your face and your jaw. Close your eyes.

- Inhale through the nose for a count of four.
- Pause and hold the breath in for a count of seven.
- Exhale fully for a count of eight.
- Continue this sequence for three minutes.

JOURNALING

- Where do you feel you lack discipline in your life? Choose one of the following areas to journal about: nutrition, sleep, spiritual practice, morning routine, time management, follow-up with friends and family, physical activities, learnings, etc.

TAKE ACTION

- To bring more discipline into your life, (to be able to listen to your true needs and find balance), what do you need to stop doing and what do you need to start doing? Start making changes within twenty-four hours and follow up within a month. For example, two nights a week I do not watch television or spend time on my computer. Instead, I read or have conversations with friends or family.

BE ECOLOGICAL

Hold on! We are not trying to fit this topic in because it is trendy or because it looks good. Our purpose is to constantly help you connect to your true identity. Ecology is another way to understand who we are.

Ecology is the study of relationships between organisms including humans, animals, and their physical environment. When we are aware of the consequences each system has on another, we become more respectful and more mindful.

To do so, we must remember a few things: we are not living *on* earth; we are living *in* earth. We are the planet. We are the earth as much as the trees, the plants, the animals, and the oxygen.

There is an intrinsic dance between plants and us. Plants provide oxygen for humans, and humans provide carbon dioxide that is absorbed by plants. Thus, without one another, neither would survive.

This earth has a limited amount of natural resources. We need to stop assuming innovation will always bail us out of the ongoing destruction we generate. We need to realize the damage to the earth is our problem, and the problem of future generations. Therefore, we need to treat the earth and its resources with respect and minimalism, in order to preserve them for future generations.

When you choose to educate yourself and explore how you can reduce your ecological footprint, you open your heart differently because you realize how sacred and precious everything is. You recognize there is an ongoing interconnectedness with everything. You realize it is not me versus them; it is we.

When you develop a global awareness, you become a citizen of the earth first. Your country of origin, your community, your religion, your political affiliation must come second. It does not mean you have to solve every problem, but you do have to pay attention. Everything counts; every thought, every word, every action counts.

When the act of caring is at the center of your lifestyle, the mind slows down, perhaps even your blood pressure will slow down, and your heart will expand. This will allow you to connect more specifically and purposefully with everyone and everything around you.

Take time to pause and connect to all that is around you: the wind, the fragrances, the sounds, the light, etc. Don't wait for your next vacation to appreciate your surroundings. Don't wait for a law or a political ruling to start respecting the earth. Start today using the knowledge and spirit within you.

THE PRACTICE
MEDITATION: TREE POSE
You may consider Tree Pose as a meditation practice. Tree pose invites you to stay focused; it will improve your stability and your balance at the physical, emotional, mental, and spiritual levels.

- Begin standing with your arms at your sides. Distribute your weight evenly on your feet.
- Visualize yourself as a tree.
- Shift your weight to your left foot and depending on your abilities, lift your right foot and place it on your left shin or thigh.
- Place your hands on your hips, or in prayer position in front of your heart center.
- Gaze softly at an unmoving point in front of you.
- If you feel balanced, lift your hands toward the sky, arms open or in prayer position.
- Hold the position or continue to come back into it for one minute.
- Repeat on the opposite side.

JOURNALING

- Pick one of the following: a rock, a tree, the ocean, or the sky. Journal from their perspective about their experience. What is it like to be a tree, the sky, etc.?

TAKE ACTION

- Commit to reducing your ecological footprint and/or celebrating your surroundings. To get started: Consider planting a tree or bringing your own bag when you go shopping.

Be Empty

Being empty usually means we are depleted or exhausted and our ability to bounce back is gone. We may feel there is something missing. We can be empty in many ways: physically (such as hunger), mentally (as in a sense of being drained or without anything to offer), and spiritually (as in feeling lost and alone).

In business, if your schedule is full, you are good at what you do. Many company cultures encourage long hours and constant pressure to be successful.

At home, becoming an empty nester is often perceived as a problem to solve. Our clients who are faced with this situation experience loss: they need to shift and patiently rediscover purpose as they allow this transition to unfold.

Many cultures do not promote the art of emptiness, because as we buy less our economic model cringes.

Especially as Americans, we are often caught up in buying more and thinking more is better. We don't stop and think that maybe sometimes less is best. Many holidays have now become about gifts: getting the best deal or the newest "toy" seems to be the path to happiness.

Every time we celebrate, we create a notion of abundance by providing too much. Too much food, too much wine, too many gifts, and we leave the table full, which generates apathy. We never promote space for "nothingness," even though it is a way to gain clarity and a new perspective.

In America, obesity is an epidemic. For example, in 2016, 40% of adults and 30% of children were obese. Overeating results in many deaths. To be alive, practice emptiness.

If your physical body is constantly full, it cannot do its necessary cleansing; your energy lessens, and your ability to focus is compromised. Now consider your breath: if you are full you cannot breathe deeply. When you don't breathe deeply, your health is negatively impacted.

Beyond the physical body, pay attention to how you live. Clear your space. Also, clear your emotions. If you hold on to unprocessed and unresolved feelings, there is no room for listening, reaching out, or connecting. Space (emptiness) is the foundation for your creativity and imagination to blossom. The mind by nature generates many thoughts. *Modern Psychology* estimates that we have 70,000 thoughts per day and the yogis believe we have 1000 thoughts per blink of an eye. Regardless of the exact number, you must clear your mind if you want clarity and stability. One way to do this is with meditation. In fact, one purpose of meditation is to empty the mind.

The heart, by nature, cannot be too full, simply because love is space, love is flow, and love is about sharing. Practice the beginner's mind, in which you are not carrying any preconceived ideas, and you stay open.

Be empty; you will realize that nothing is missing or lacking.

PRACTICE

MEDITATION: FOLLOW THE MIND

This meditation helps you create an experience of emptiness. The more you follow your thoughts and their ramifications, the emptier you will feel.

- Sit in a comfortable position. Lengthen your spine and draw your shoulders down your back. Soften your face and your jaw. Close your eyes.
- To the best of your ability track and follow your thoughts.
- Stay focused and keep pursuing your thoughts.
- Continue this process for three minutes and notice how you feel.

JOURNALING

- Assess your relationship with emptiness. How much emptiness do you allow in your life? What emotions arise when you allow emptiness to be part of your life? As an example, explore the following areas:
  - Your relationship with time. Do you allow space and time for self, without an agenda?

- Your relationship with food. Do you leave a meal full or with 1/3 of your belly empty?

TAKE ACTION

- Decide to clear a space: your closet, your car, your living room, your office, etc. Notice the changes it creates within you.
- Clear your schedule. Allow enough space on a weekly basis for some quiet time with yourself.

BE FREE

Being free is not about doing whatever you want whenever you want; it is not about having it your way. Being free is accepting yourself unconditionally.

When is being you enough? When being you is not locked into a specific image you believe you need to project to be accepted, admired, or loved, then you are free. When you acknowledge your gifts and limitations and can appreciate all of you, you are free. You are free to be a mosaic of thoughts, ideas, and values.

When you are free you experience every emotion. You are not blocking or denying some feelings because they are too painful or because you want to appear a certain way. You are authentic with your sensations and therefore, authentic with you; your inside matches your outside.

You are not on earth to be understood. When you want to be understood, you may start bending, compromising, adjusting, or apologizing. You are not on earth to convince people to go your way and follow your path. As soon as you try to convince others, you create attachments. This is not to say that compromise and apologizing are unnecessary. The focus here is to go within, explore your own individuality, and take the risk of expressing your own voice without the fear of judgement.

Freedom brings a nurturing quality as we tune into our life pulse. Inner freedom takes work; it requires patience and inquiry. Stay curious as you explore and discover your patterns. Are you holding on to your past, your present, and/or your future? Are you attached to being right? Are you caught up in pain or pleasure? Are you able to forgive? Are you consumed by expectations of yourself and others?

The path of freedom is the path of personal growth, the path of healing and awareness, the path of expressing your destiny where you honor your unique self and create your own trail. It takes courage and it takes heart to lead like a constant seeker, never right or wrong, always open. Freedom is your birthright.

THE PRACTICE

MEDITATION: I AM FREE

The purpose of this meditation is to let go of any attachments by practicing a long exhale and combining a simple mantra and mudra (hand position) that support the mind to surrender. The lotus mudra helps to find your own voice by releasing tension and opening the heart.

- Sit in a comfortable position. Lengthen your spine and draw your shoulders down your back. Soften your face and your jaw. Close your eyes.
- Bend your arms to the side and bring your hands in lotus mudra by your heart center, the center of your chest. Bring the base of both hands together and connect both thumbs and pinkie fingers.
- Take a deep breath in through the nose.
- On the exhale, out loud in a monotone way, repeat the mantra six to eight times: "I am free. I am, I am."
- Continue for three minutes.

JOURNALING

- Make a list of attachments from your past, present, and future. What do you need to let go of in order to feel freer?

TAKE ACTION

- Who do you need to forgive? Choose one person and reach out to them.

BE GENEROUS

Generosity is perhaps one of the best and most uplifting medicines on earth. Many studies have shown that selfless giving lowers depression and stress.

You may automatically think of generosity as a way to give your time, your money, your talents, and/or any of your available resources. It is not what or how much you are giving, but rather how mindful and present you are. True generosity embodies unity and freedom. Your presence itself can be generous.

Alyson, Shari's close friend and mentor, has been giving money to homeless people for many years. One day, she realized she was not making eye contact when giving the money. She now takes time to connect and be present as she gives. This new way of being generous helped her open her heart.

When you give, while also staying fully present, your whole body opens. At that moment you receive as much as you give; you are creating a new you, you are transforming yourself. Generosity becomes an alchemical process.

Beyond giving, consider receiving an important aspect of generosity. When you embrace someone fully and allow that person the space to unfold, you are generous. Receiving is not taking; it is accepting and recognizing the other. At that moment, your whole body relaxes and opens; your heart creates a nurturing space for anyone and anything.

It is easier to be generous when "life is good." When a crisis occurs, you may go into fear mode and disconnect from generosity. Most likely, you will become territorial in all aspects of your life, thus losing your joy and vitality.

Being generous means believing abundance is part of life. When this paradigm becomes your foundation, you will be more relaxed, present, and able to celebrate.

Kindra, one of Tejpal's clients, has been unhappy for the past few years in her job as an engineer. Kindra comes from a family who struggled financially, and therefore, she believes she should stay in her job position no matter what. As she started to heal her fear of lacking, Kindra was then able to move beyond her limiting beliefs and contact several headhunters. She is now starting a new job in a different organization. Still struggling with her fear of failure, Kindra chose to celebrate her transition, even if her future is not guaranteed.

At times it seems we have nothing left to give, and this can lead to feelings of guilt. It is important to set boundaries and practice generosity for self, despite cultural or societal pressure. Being generous to self goes beyond a spa day; this introspective process requires identifying and addressing your needs and desires. For example, Sarah, one of Shari's clients, is a mother of four boys between the ages of eight and fourteen. She started the therapy session sharing the fact that she was extremely irritated with everything. Sarah did not know how to take care of her own needs; she never took the time to eat and was always on the go. She also did not spend enough time doing the things she loved: being in nature and with animals. As she started to slowly change her lifestyle and be generous in all aspects, she was able to have more compassion for herself and others.

If your generosity is driven by ego, your need for recognition, prestige, or status will lead the show. On the outside, you look good, but on the inside you feel disconnected. Take the time to check in regarding your intention.

Call on your playfulness, authenticity, and creativity to express your generosity. It is not a duty, but a doorway to the revival of your full self. The more you give, the more vibrant you become!

THE PRACTICE

MEDITATION: LOVING KINDNESS

The purpose of this meditation is to open your heart to oneself and others. The practice of repetition and focus in this meditation encourages sensitivity and compassion, which will continue throughout the day.

- Sit in a comfortable position. Lengthen your spine and draw your shoulders down your back. Soften your face and your jaw. Close your eyes.

- Take a few breaths and focus on relaxing the center of your chest, the area of your heart center.

- First practice toward oneself. Slowly and steadily, mentally repeat the following phrase: May I be happy. May I be well. May I be safe. May I be peaceful and at ease. The intention of this practice is to cultivate well-being and ease; stay present to what arises. Do this a minimum of five times.

- Then think of a loved one, a family member, or a friend. Slowly, mentally repeat the same phrases with the person/persons in mind: May you be happy. May you be well. May you be safe. May you be peaceful and at ease.

- Next, bring to mind a person you have difficulty with. Slowly and mentally repeat the same phrase: May (name)_____be happy. May_____be well. May_____be safe. May_____ be peaceful and at ease.

- Next, bring to mind the world around; animals, nature, and all beings: May all beings be happy. May all beings be well. May all beings be safe. May all beings be peaceful and at ease.

JOURNALING

- What limits your generosity?
- In what areas of your life would you like to be more generous?

TAKE ACTION

- Practice generosity in a way you have not done before. Whether you cook, mentor, drive someone to an appointment, etc. Add a new dimension to what you already do. For example, if you cook for a friend who had surgery, you may want to set the table.

BE HEALTHY

Don't worry, we are not giving a lecture on what you should eat or how many hours you should sleep, and we are not coming up with a new diet. Then what are we focusing on?

Health has nothing to do with being perfect; it has to do with creating flow no matter what happens in your life. If you are traveling and your flight is delayed, if a loved one is ill, if you simply feel exhausted, are you able to be healthy? Are you able to adapt to the constant changes? Are you able to be creative enough to design a life balance at the physical, emotional, mental, and spiritual levels?

We tend to fall into a routine in our lives, and eventually, the routine owns us. At that moment, we have lost our life force. There is a tendency to go a step further and become addicted to a routine, to the point that it becomes a fixation. Our life choices may look healthy at first: we have a workout program and eating and sleeping regimes that may generate a lot of respect, yet, we become obsessed with it. When our lifestyle takes over our relationships and creates separation from the rest of the world, we are unhealthy. When we become rigid with our choices, we open the door to diseases.

When you are healthy, you have more than one gear; you are not stuck in one pattern. At the physical level, we know that nutrition and diversity in our movements are key to health and vitality. The healthier you are, the easier it is to adapt. If you are used to a specific morning routine, can you simply go for a daily walk when you are away from home?

Following guidelines for your health is certainly beneficial, yet you are the one to decide and design what is healthy for you. When you choose to be healthy, you choose to awaken the healer within, the one that is able to nourish oneself no matter what the circumstances. There will be days or weeks where your life will be out of balance. If you are healthy, you will feel it, recognize it, and eventually be able to create a new level of health.

Being healthy is not about doing it right necessarily; it is about forgiving yourself, letting go, and always fine-tuning your lifestyle so you can stay in the flow.

Pleasure is an important aspect of health, yet, becoming healthier may not be pleasurable in the beginning. Your body and mind will resist any changes. For this reason, when creating a new level of health at the physical, emotional, mental, heart, and spiritual levels, you will need a support system during the early stages of transformation.

Your health is the foundation for your happiness. It impacts how you think and how you feel. Take advantage of it.

THE PRACTICE

MEDITATION: MOVING BREATH

The purpose of this meditation is to connect breath with movements and strengthen the heart while staying grounded. It engages and unifies the whole body, heart, and mind, which is the essence of yoga. Yoga comes from the word "yoke", which means unifying. In this case, unifying mind, body, and spirit.

- Begin by standing, arms by your side, gaze soft or eyes closed. Take a moment to connect to your breath.
- Inhale through the nose and bring your arms out to the side, palms facing down. Draw your shoulders down your back. Exhale through the nose and bring your hands together in prayer position, in front of your heart center.
- Inhale through the nose and lift your hands toward the sky. Turn your gaze up. Exhale through the nose, turn your palms out and slowly lower your arms back down by your side.
- Repeat the sequence for three minutes.

JOURNALING

Here are five domains to look at:

- Sleep/Rest
- Nutrition
- Physical Activities
- Relationships
- Stress Level

Choose one of the five domains listed above. Journal about creative ways to maintain or implement

healthy life choices, no matter what the circumstances are.

TAKE ACTION: SELF-ASSESSMENT

- On a scale of 1 to 10, rate your level of health
  in the five domains listed above (10 being op-
  timal). Identify and implement a change in
  one domain at a time.

BE HOPELESS

We do not take pleasure in your misery, nor are we interested in bringing you down. Being hopeful holds beautiful possibilities; it allows you to dream and use your imagination to create a better world. Hope has a powerful energy that can nurture you through any crisis. Hope can be the magic that helps you endure and overcome obstacles.

Sometimes hope fabricates a veil and prevents you from seeing your current situation clearly. There is a tendency to disconnect, go into "la la land," and avoid addressing difficult conversations or making courageous decisions.

The practice of being hopeless reminds you to be present to what is. It also encourages you not to hide in an ideal, fantasy future. It invites you to take specific action now, instead of procrastinating and hoping things will get better on their own.

By being hopeless, you let go of specific expectations and choose not to count on an imaginary future. When hope takes over your life, you hide in your head and stop making necessary changes to better yourself. If hope were a good excuse not to change anything, while expecting different results, then it would resemble the well-known definition of insanity.

The practice of being hopeless is a reset and an opportunity to step away from any attachment about your future. The promise lies in your spirit, the present, and the actions you are taking.

Cultivating the art of hopelessness allows you to embrace the true gifts of hopefulness. Being hopeful is not about avoiding your reality by going into dreamland and clinging to unrealistic expectations. By practicing hopelessness, you will learn that the energy of hope starts at the heart center and shines a unique light, allowing you to uplift yourself and others.

Take advantage of being hopeless; it is a necessary wakeup call that reminds you of the fragility, instability, and impermanence of life. It will give you the courage to stay honest with what is, and help you become more engaged in your life.

THE PRACTICE

MEDITATION: ALTERNATE NOSTRIL BREATHING

The purpose of this practice is to balance both hemispheres of the brain and help you be more centered and energized. This new foundation helps you accept every situation with ease.

- Sit in a comfortable position. Lengthen your spine and draw your shoulders down your back. Soften your face and your jaw. Close your eyes.
- Take a couple of breaths to center.
- Rest your index and middle fingers on the bridge of your nose.
- Use your right thumb to block your right nostril and inhale through the left nostril.
- Block the left nostril with your ring and pinkie fingers, release your right thumb and exhale through the right nostril.
- Keep blocking your left nostril and inhale through the right nostril.

- Then block the right nostril with your right thumb, release ring and pinky fingers and exhale through the left nostril.
- Continue for three minutes.

JOURNALING

- Remember a situation that brought nagging discomfort. Where did your mind go? Did it go to an extreme, such as defeat mode, or result in a happy resolution? Were you able to be more neutral and/or hopeless? Think of ways you could have approached it differently.

TAKE ACTION

- Choose an activity where you are not attached to the outcome, such as working in the yard, doing arts and crafts projects, or going for a walk while allowing your mind to wander.

BE A HOST

If you want to live healthy, happy, and holy, become a host for everything in your life, the good and the bad. When you host a problem, instead of pushing it away, you may realize it becomes more manageable. Often the real problem is not the problem itself, but how you relate to it. If you host an illness, the energy will run its course and you may benefit from it. You will not become worse and you may gain some insight. The path of healing is about embracing your light and your shadow. Every time you try to push things away, contain them, or control them, you don't learn, and you don't grow. Every time you create a wall, you create fear.

Jackie is involved in many projects and carries a lot of responsibility on her shoulders. When she came to our workshop she was overwhelmed with anxiety and believed her emotions were linked to the nature of her work. She realized her anxiety had little to do with any outside event. When she understood this pattern had been within her for a long time, she became very depressed. By allowing herself to relate to the anxiety and hosting it, she was able to start her healing process. She now has a meditation practice and can delegate projects at work with ease.

Be a host for what you have and what you don't have. It is only when we host that transformation happens. Be a host for your joy and your sadness, in order to stay authentic. Be a host for other's joy and pain, so that they can find their inner stability again.

There is only one part of you that truly knows what hosting is all about: your heart. Your heart connects to your infinite self and is the organ with the biggest energy field. When you host from your heart, you have no intention of taking any action or giving advice; you listen to nourish.

When you host from the heart, you are detached from any outcomes. Instead of telling people what to do, you allow them to create their own path so they can connect to their true identity. Every time we make demands of someone, it may prevent them from connecting to who they truly are.

We spend so much time wanting things our way that when we don't get our way, we may shut down, become depressed, impatient, frustrated, lethargic, or angry. Our inability to accept "what is" generates a constant fight within us. When we are caught in conflict, we are pulled in many directions; we are not centered or grounded. We can't welcome anything, and we ignore what love is all about: being a host for everything.

When you choose to be an unconditional host, you drop your resistance and your emotional self deflates. By doing so, you are neither running away nor running toward, and you experience one of the most precious qualities on earth: peace.

THE PRACTICE

MEDITATION:
WELCOMING AND INVITING

This meditation helps you notice the strong connections between mind, emotions, and physical body. It encourages you to stay present and feel your experience of what arises.

- Sit in a comfortable position, close your eyes, and imagine a joyful experience. Notice your breath: Is it fast or slow, deep or shallow? Is it smooth or scattered? Notice how your body feels. Where do you feel a flow, and where do you feel constricted? What parts of your body feel vibrant?
- Close your eyes again and connect to a challenging situation. Notice your breath: Is it fast or slow, deep or shallow? Is it smooth or scattered? Notice how your body feels. Where do you feel a flow, and where do you feel constricted? What parts of your body feel vibrant?
- Now sit and notice your natural breath. Don't try to change it. Were you able to welcome both experiences? How do you feel at this moment?

JOURNALING

- What is the most difficult emotion for you to welcome? How do you resist and/or avoid it?

What is your coping mechanism for that particular emotion?

TAKE ACTION

- Now that you have identified a difficult emotion, express it. Examples could be drawing, dancing, painting, attending a kick boxing class, or writing a song.

BE INSPIRATIONAL

How do you inspire? By being courageous, heroic, or uplifting? The road to inspiring does not lead to perfection. When you are inspired you are deeply touched: your breath changes, your energy shifts, you pause, and at that moment, you are present.

Inspiration has little to do with motivation. When you inspire, you touch the heart; when you motivate, you engage the will. Also, inspiring is not the same as convincing. When you convince you push through, you force others to look at things a certain way; you are attached to a specific outcome. When you inspire, you elevate others and let them be. There is no attachment to the results. Inspiring also has nothing to do with impressing others. When you impress, your ego leads.

Inspiring starts at a quiet place within; there is no big flag to carry, no tag line on your forehead; it starts deep in your heart. It is the combination of your vulnerability and your resilience; it is a blend of fragility and courage. When you inspire, your heart is pure and authentic. You can use every experience as a teaching opportunity.

Inspire comes from the Latin, *inspirare*, which means breathe or blow into. Inspiring brings your breath to the center, not your mind or your agenda. Your breath is your life force; it is what makes you vibrant and healthy. Breath builds your prana, which is an important energy body in the yogic tradition; without prana, there is no physical body. Without inspiration, there is no elevation, no magic, and no transformation. Inspiration allows you to go beyond duality, beyond your physical limitations; it taps into the divine.

When you realize inspiring has nothing to do with accomplishing or conquering, but everything to do with awakening through the subtle touch of the heart; then you know that you do not need to be big to inspire, only authentic and constantly open to learning.

To inspire, breathe and put yourself aside; drop your ego and let your breath take over your mind. Explore both aspects of inspiration, the giving and the receiving. Listen deeply and allow yourself to be inspired by your surroundings and people's lives. Take the risk to inspire and to be seen as fragile and unsure, willing to go beyond your comfort zone to touch the heart of others. Give for no reason, in a way that touches you. Surrender to your breath, and at that very moment, you will be inspired, and you will be able to inspire as well.

THE PRACTICE
MEDITATION: CLEARING BREATH

The purpose of this meditation is to generate energy and clear the mind. You will feel uplifted and relaxed at the same time. By bringing your hands in prayer position, you balance the right and left hemispheres of the brain.

- Sit in a comfortable position. Lengthen your spine and draw your shoulders down your back. Soften your face and your jaw. Close your eyes and focus on the brow point.
- Bring your hands in prayer position.

- Inhale four times (four segmented breaths without exhaling) through the nose.
- Exhale four times (four segmented breaths without inhaling) through the nose.
- Each segmented breath should be approximately one second.
- Repeat this cycle for three minutes.

JOURNALING

- Think of someone who inspired/inspires you: this person can be living or deceased, famous or familiar; it could be anyone.
- Write a letter to that person, letting them know how they inspired you, regardless if the person is alive or not. You do not have to physically send the letter.

TAKE ACTION

- Choose to be inspired and inspire every day for one week.
- Everyday, take a picture that inspires you and send it to a loved one.
- Everyday, read a poem or a quote and share your insights with others.

BE INTELLIGENT

D on't stress over this one, and don't assume you have it either. The intelligence we are looking for is not related to what you know or what you have achieved.

At the beginning of the 20th century, the Intelligence Quotient (I.Q.) test was born: the focus was on short-term memory, analytical thinking, and mathematical and spatial abilities. It was about how quickly and flexible the mind could embrace conceptual information and solve problems. In the 1990s, we realized social intelligence was necessary to generate success and happiness, and thus the Emotional Intelligence (E.Q.) test was born. This test focused on the ability to assess emotions and make appropriate decisions. In the late nineties, we started to focus on a new form of intelligence: spiritual intelligence, which has been defined using a vast range of criteria. Some refer to spiritual intelligence as mindfulness (the ability to be present), self-awareness, and humility, to name a few. We also have Artificial Intelligence (A. I.), which uses computer technology to assimilate a vast range of information to create specific actions and predict results.

What we are interested in is your heart intelligence. The heart is a complex organ with an energy field 5000 times bigger than the energy field of the brain. When your heart is vibrant, its energy field shifts, changes, and assimilates a wide range of information. The Heart Rate Variability, known as HRV, looks at the fluctuation of your heart between heartbeats. The higher the rate, the more fluctuation your heart has between beats, and the more vibrant you are. As you age, or if you have a deficiency in your heart, your HRV will go down.

Following the patterns of your heart, the intelligence we are looking for is the one that keeps you vibrant, the one that allows you to process a wide range of information and constantly adapt. As soon as you become rigid, as soon as you narrow your experience, or as soon as you create tunnel vision, your intelligence lessens.

When you are curious, evolving, and able to adapt, you are intelligent. When you can accept what is, instead of being attached to what could be, you are intelligent. You learn to embrace the unknown, dance with unpredictability, and bounce back when things don't go your way. Everything becomes an opportunity for personal growth.

At times it is important to recognize when we are not intelligent. Tejpal, who is passionate about many forms of art, went to a musical expecting to be bored. It was a Friday night show after a long week of work. If she had not bought the tickets and already committed to a friend, she would have skipped it. Yet, she was blown away by the performance and truly taken by surprise. She realized how shut down and limited she was.

Developing your flexibility and embracing diversity are at the core of the heart intelligence. By keeping a beginner's mind and staying open, you cultivate heart intelligence and embrace life and its many adventures.

THE PRACTICE

MEDITATION: BREATH OF FIRE

A clear and vibrant body will help you develop your curiosity and flexibility. The purpose of this breath is to strengthen the nervous system and the immune system. Do this breath on an empty stomach. Avoid this breath if you are in your moon cycle or if you are over four months pregnant.

- Breath of fire is a panting breath that engages the belly. First, bring your dominant hand over your navel. Inhale through an open mouth and bring your belly out (your hand on your belly is here to help you monitor your breath at the beginning). As you exhale, squeeze the belly to let the air out. Repeat the process and pick up the pace. If you are uncomfortable doing it with your mouth open, close your mouth and do the same inhale and exhale through the nose.
- Do this breath for three minutes.

JOURNALING

- Make a list of how your lifestyle encourages diversity of cultures, activities, and opportunities.

- Journal about your lack of intelligence in certain situations. Notice your patterns. It could be about your quick judgments, or strong opinions, or inabilities to open up to something you don't understand, etc.

TAKE ACTION

- Every year stretch yourself and explore new activities. For example: participating in a new dance class, reading a book on a topic you know nothing about, joining a new community event, exploring a new style of cooking, or going back to school.

BE INTUITIVE

Intuition is not about super power; it is not ego or magic centered. It is the truest form of service to self and others. No matter what your skill set, you are born with intuition. Pay attention to your intention and integrity: check your ego and align. If you are here to brag about your intuition and pretend you know something others do not, if you think you are special because you can master that gift, then let it go.

Intuition starts with a simple principle taught by many spiritual teachers thousands of years ago: the principle that everything is energy. What is perceived as solid is in fact made of 99.99% space. Our thoughts and emotions are energy. When you embrace this paradigm that is now well accepted in the field of quantum physics, you can relate to everything energetically. You can connect to the essence of everything, beyond what you see at the physical level; your intuitive self is now guiding you through life.

You may believe that in order to connect to the non-physical, you need to leave your physical body and be in your head. The danger in this is that you will go into projections and fantasies.

To connect to the energy of everything, you need to go deeper into your body. Close your eyes, slow your breath, and pay attention to your sensations and emotions throughout the body without trying to make sense of your experience. At that moment the mind is not controlling, and you can experience wholeness, the foundation of intuition. At that moment you are fully present in the now.

You may resist going into your body due to past challenges. You may be preventing yourself from tuning in and exploring your sensory system. Your past traumas may be in the way of trusting your body and relying on the information you receive. You may not be able to discern whether your experience comes from a place of fear and reaction or from a place of intuition.

Be patient and first practice with situations in which you are not attached to the outcomes, as this will allow you to stay neutral. A simple way to practice could be to try on an old friend or a family member you have not been in touch with for a long time.

As you close your eyes, imagine that person sitting beside you. Imagine you are a host welcoming that person into your body. Scan your body, pay attention to your emotions and physical sensations. Then, whatever your findings are, reach out to that person and inquire as to how they are doing.

You may be attached to facts and figures and believe that the sciences are the only answer.

But, let's face it, we once thought Earth was the center of the universe, vitamin C was "it," and the list goes on. Sciences serve many purposes and we can be extremely grateful for them. Yet, they are limited and often obsolete. As soon as we discover something, there will be new research to expand or challenge the current findings.

Instead of becoming excited about new trends and discoveries, instead of jumping in and following any impulse you may have, pause and check in. When intuition guides your decisions and actions, you become more unified and in harmony with your surroundings. Intuition is your best asset.

THE PRACTICE

MEDITATION: CLEAR THE MIND

A longer exhale will stimulate the para-sympathetic nervous system, which supports relaxation and prevents you from going into fight or flight mode. As you become less reactive, it will be easier to develop your intuition.

- Sit in a comfortable position. Lengthen your spine and draw your shoulders down your back. Soften your face and your jaw. Close your eyes and look up; focus on the brow point.
- Inhale through the nose for a count of 6 and hold the breath in for a count of 6
- Exhale slowly through the nose for a count of 12 (if that is too challenging for you, start with inhaling for a count of 4, hold for a count of 4 and exhale for a count of 8).

- Bring your hands on your lap in Gyan mudra: press your thumb and index finger together in each hand.
- Continue for three minutes.

JOURNALING

- Every day for a week, answer the following question: How can I create more stillness and relaxation in my life?

TAKE ACTION

- Go outside and choose something to practice on. It can be a rock, a plant, a flower, or a tree.
- Bringing the quality of stillness, connect to what you chose with all your senses.
- Close your eyes and slow your breath.
- Relax, soften, and drop into your body.
- Be receptive with all your senses; pay attention to the patterns within your body.
- What did you notice?

BE INVINCIBLE

You don't need to be superwoman, superman, or a superhero to be invincible. You need to change your beliefs and focus on one thing: your true self.

You are born in a physical body that comes and goes; your true self is your essence. It never changes; it reflects your intrinsic qualities. It has nothing to do with your age, gender, or roles. It is you.

The more we stay in touch with who we truly are, the more stable we become. Nothing can shake us; we are strong from within. When we lose our connection to our true self, our circumstances dictate our confidence and concept of self. We either go into crisis and doer mode (trying to fix, solve or manage everything that comes our way), or we may give up and go into victimhood. We will never be satisfied, always worried and anxious about what the future may bring.

When you stay in touch with your true self, losses, rejections, failures, and victories are simply learning experiences. If you want joy and serenity, you need to align with your essence.

There is a natural tendency to disconnect. It is easy to reject challenges; the more we deny or ignore the unwanted, the further away from our true self we get. By being invincible, like a true spiritual warrior, we acknowledge and face any adversity. It does not mean that we will conquer what comes to us; we will, however, move through with love and conviction. Ignorance and giving up are not an option.

Being invincible is believing in and committing to who we truly are. If you want to stay connected to you, bring joy into your life. It is as essential to your core as water and food. Joy is vitamin D for the soul. You may believe you don't have time for this: you want to be sure your bills are paid, your house is cleaned, your kids do their homework, and the list goes on. All these items are important, yet, if you are constantly in do mode, attached to your checklist, you will eventually lose your sense of self. The problem is you believe this is your only option, but really what are you avoiding? Joy is not a luxury; you don't have to be wealthy to bring joy to your life.

Be invincible; commit to nurture your true self, even in chaotic situations, so that peace and balance remain at the center of your life.

THE PRACTICE

MEDITATION: WARRIOR POSE

The purpose of this meditation is to increase balance, focus and stability.

- Start standing and take a few breaths as you connect to your spiritual warrior.
- Take a wide stance.
- Turn your right toes in and your left toes out towards 90 degrees.
- Inhale and raise your arms to shoulder level, palms facing down; exhale as you draw your shoulders down your back.
- Inhale and with the next exhalation bend the left knee and gaze over your left fingertips.
- Evenly distribute your weight and engage

your core, Stay in this position for three to five breaths.

- Reverse the position of the feet and repeat on the other side.

JOURNALING

- Make a list of what brings you joy. For example: singing, spending time with loved ones or being in nature.

TAKE ACTION

- Choose one element of your list and incorporate it into your life.
- Take a hike, join a choir, or go to a concert.

Be Kind

When you choose kindness as a way of living, your breath pattern automatically changes and your tempo shifts. Everything inside of you slows down and softens. You become more relaxed, and with this, more present and aware of what is going on within you and around you.

Many studies have been done about the benefits of kindness: our blood pressure decreases, our heart rate slows down, and our nervous system relaxes.

There are also some significant benefits at the emotional level. Forty million adults in America are affected by depression and anxiety. One of the roots of this emotional distress is the lack of meaningful and nourishing connections. Kindness reminds us of the importance of relationships. The magic of this world lies in how we relate to one another and ourselves. Kindness invites the other to unfold in their unique way, which is not necessarily predictable. There is no demand, no pressure, but there is space and respect.

In communication, kindness is a game changer in the way we hear and are heard. When you speak from kindness you soften, and your message will be heard and received differently. When you chose to listen with kindness, you are listening from your heart, a place of openness and acceptance.

Kindness does not prevent difficult situations, but it can help with addressing challenges. You don't have to be sweet, hold back, or be a pleaser; you can share your truth in a kind way. Confronting, setting boundaries, or speaking up is sometimes necessary, even if it may not be well received. Kindness will not stop the pain, but it will help you speak from a place of inner stability and clarity that is not reactive.

Without kindness, our thoughts and behaviors solidify and encourage black and white thinking. Kindness is a dance of flexibility, fluidity, and compassion. Kindness is contagious: smile at a stranger and, most of the time, they will smile back at you. That simple gesture of reaching out will uplift you.

Choose kindness; become a host for yourself and others, and your spirit will brighten.

THE PRACTICE

MEDITATION: INNER SMILE MEDITATION

The purpose of inner smile meditation is to activate the energy of loving-kindness within us. It comes from the Taoist tradition.

- Sit in a comfortable position. Lengthen your spine and draw your shoulders down your back. Soften your face and your jaw. Close your eyes.
- Imagine that every cell in your body is smiling. You have over 32 trillion cells.
- Keep smiling without smiling with your lips.
- Continue this practice for a minimum of three minutes.

JOURNALING

- Keep a kindness journal and every day write acts of kindness you have witnessed or expressed.

TAKE ACTION

- Smile at every stranger for a whole day, at the gas station, at the grocery store, over the phone, etc. Just smile first.
- Choose to wake up with kindness.

BE LESS

For many years the American culture has promoted the concept of being more and having more. This notion of having more is fueled by competitiveness and insecurity. Our energy focuses on keeping an eye on our neighbors and friends to make sure they aren't getting ahead of us or gaining "more" than us. Thus, the popular saying, "Keeping up with the Joneses."

Some aspects of this notion are useful, as they support the idea that each human being has tremendous potential, as well as acknowledging that we often limit ourselves. But when being more became the American dream and, in a way, the national anthem, we found ourselves in trouble, as "more" turned into a value to constantly aim for.

When more is at the center of your life, you are completely disconnected from your true self. You are agitated, excited, or anxious about the gap between what you have and how much more you may get. When you focus on more, the what and the who are confused. If you have more, you think you *are* more, and that is perceived as success. Chasing more gives you a false sense of security and purpose.

One of our clients, John, was a successful lawyer in his mid-forties. He was a partner in his firm, had a beautiful home, and a lavish lifestyle. Recently, he developed major depression, to the point of not being able to work. John's drive to have more and to be more came to a halt. His having more felt meaningless. John decided to change his lifestyle and engage in new activities that brought him joy. His needs changed and now that he is back at work he has chosen to work less and is open to new possibilities. John is no longer chasing the dream of more and bigger. He has realized these things do not make him happy or fulfilled. He has connected with his true self and is now living for what feeds his soul and not his wallet.

What if you looked at the gifts of being less? What if being less invited you to have less ego, less pride, less attachment, and less of your persona, so your true self could be less distracted and obsessed? What if you did not need to own or do more so you could feel more at peace?

Being less invites you to be quiet. When this happens, your spiritual self expands, and you are able to look at everything that comes to you as a gift, as a blessing. Be less and bless. A gift does not mean you have to smile. A gift means that no matter what pain or suffering you are going through, if you are willing to embrace it, eventually your heart will soften and expand.

It is believed that in the 6th century, Pope Gregory I suggested saying "God Bless You" after a person sneezed, in hopes this prayer would protect them from dying. When you choose to be less and bless, your mind shifts and stays away from drama. Many spiritual practices include blessing rituals. Some bless the four directions, our ancestors, nature, a newborn, a meal, a person, or a situation. Today you do not have to be a saint, a rabbi, a shaman, or a guru of any kind; you don't have to be so-called elevated and pray or meditate three hours a day to bless anyone or anything. You only need to be you, and your blessings do not have to be ceremonial. They can be quiet and discrete. Some examples of blessings are finding a small rock during a hike with friends and bringing it home as a remembrance of that special experience, framing a picture of loved ones that makes you smile, or keeping a gratitude journal.

Tejpal always starts her day by picking an angel card; she has a set in two different rooms. When she works with clients face to face, or over the phone, she always starts with a breath in order to center herself.

When being less becomes your discipline, your mindset and your spirit stay away from commotion. You can embrace and appreciate what you have and who you are, instead of running after something you do not have; you can connect to your holiness within, which simply means you are healthy, happy, and whole.

THE PRACTICE

MEDITATION: BLESSING

The purpose of a mantra is to help the mind slow down and focus. The repetition on the inhale and exhale serves to reset, deepen the breath, and connect to self.

- Sit in a comfortable position. Lengthen your spine and draw your shoulders down your back. Soften your face and your jaw. Close your eyes.
- Bring your hands in prayer position by your heart center, the center of your chest.
- While inhaling through the nose, mentally repeat four times: I bless myself.
- Then while exhaling through the nose, mentally repeat four times: I am, I am.
- Repeat this cycle for three minutes.

JOURNALING

- Take inventory of your personality traits, behaviors, or habits and explore where being less can help you be more authentic.

TAKE ACTION

- Create a new blessing ritual: bless your meal, bless your day, bless yourself, etc.
- Identify an area where you put too much energy, and/or time, and cut it by a third. For example, be on your phone/social media *less*.

BE LIGHT

We are not asking you to be an angel, although that would be wonderful! We are inviting you to live with a spirit full of light. To embrace this practice, let's explore two concepts: heavy versus light and dark versus light.

Heavy versus Light

When things get heavy, you are often stuck with sluggishness or depression. Even in the most challenging times of your life, heaviness is not necessary, it keeps you in the past. Lightness helps you to move on. Heaviness can prevent you from healing: you can't let go, and you can't forgive. To stay vibrant, everything needs to move and flow. Lightness allows you to dance with what is and supports your ability to bounce back. If you choose to keep it light, you are more flexible and adapt quickly to life's constant changes. You are not pretending everything is great and burying your head in the sand, rather you bring a different energy to the situation so that things can evolve.

Dark versus Light

You may think that dark is bad, and light is good. You may wish to stay away from darkness, whatever that means to you. If you spend your life avoiding darkness, you will live in fear with a lot of anxiety and rigidity. Being light is not about hoping or praying for only good things in your life. It is not about sheer will or repeating fifty times a day: "Today is going to be a great day!" Being light is about your attitude and perspective. Are you able to keep it light through challenges?

Light does not belong to the mind, but to the heart and spirit; it allows for transcendence and transformation. We are not suggesting you go into "la la land," but rather use the light for clarity and peace. If you keep it light, you will literally see better. Light also brings a spirit of moderation (light exercise, light meal, etc.) and keeps you away from addictive patterns.

Travel light (as there is no need to carry baggage from the past) so you can stay open to new opportunities and feel free.

THE PRACTICE

MEDITATION: CHAKRA BREATH

The purpose of this meditation is to energize and balance your whole body so that you can stay open and light.

- Sit in a comfortable position. Lengthen your spine and draw your shoulders down your back. Soften your face and your jaw. Close your eyes.
- Breathe in light, starting at the base of the spine, hold the breath in for 5 to 10 seconds and exhale.
- Breathe in light, below your navel, hold the breath in for 5 to 10 seconds and exhale.
- Breathe in light, to your solar plexus, hold the breath in   for 5 to 10 seconds and exhale.
- Breathe in light to your heart center, hold the breath in for 5 to 10 seconds and exhale.
- Breathe in light to your throat, hold the breath in for 5 to 10 seconds and exhale.

- Breathe in light to your third eye, hold the breath in for 5 to 10 seconds and exhale.
- Breathe in light a few inches above your head, hold the breath in for 5 to 10 seconds and exhale.
- Lastly, relax your breath and let the light radiate throughout your body.

JOURNALING

- What do you need to let go of in order to feel lighter?

TAKE ACTION

- What is one lifestyle change you can commit to in order to lighten your day? For example, what could you do differently in your morning or evening routine?

BE ON THE EDGE

Living on the edge is not the result of a nervous breakdown or a major crisis. There is no expectation for you to be edgy, agitated, and all over the place. Being on the edge develops an attitude of exploration and discovery; it is about stretching your own limitations.

If living on the edge makes you feel as if you could fall into a precipice and lose too much, then pause, step back for a moment, and assess your fears. If you are outcome driven, living on the edge may stir up anxiety. If you are a seeker, looking to connect deeper with yourself and others, then being on the edge is the answer. At that moment, you say yes to life. You are not living on autopilot, doing the same thing, and numbing yourself; you are not falling asleep, you are awake. You don't know who you are until you challenge yourself.

Instead of whining or complaining about your limitations, you have an opportunity to have fun and grow. This way of being is not fueled by adrenaline; there is attention without tension. You are alive, yet not edgy. When you live on the edge, everything is fresh.

As long as we live in human form, we will always experience fear. We may believe that if we live in a cocoon, there will be less fear or less hurt. In fact, the less risk we take, the more afraid we are. As we take chances and make mistakes, we become more resilient and hone the ability to bounce back. Being on the edge is choosing to be present and fully engaged with this big universe. The more we put ourselves out there, the more dynamic we become.

If we define ourselves by our life force, instead of our successes and failures, we realize that life is about being open to reinventing ourselves. Every time we play safe, our energy goes down. Being alive is a risk on its own. Being in love is also a risk, why not take another risk and live on the edge?

THE PRACTICE

MEDITATION: HEALING BREATH

This meditation comes from the Kundalini Yoga tradition. In addition to rebuilding your glandular system, this breath will challenge you and help you get in touch with some unfamiliar parts.

- Sit in a comfortable position. Lengthen your spine and draw your shoulders down your back. Soften your face and your jaw. Close your eyes.
- Inhale through the nose in sixteen distinct strokes.
- Exhale through the nose in sixteen distinct strokes.
- If a sixteen strokes breath is too much, start with six and work your way up to sixteen.
- Continue for three minutes.

JOURNALING

- Journal about your biggest fear and notice how it prevents you from living on the edge.

TAKE ACTION

- At the physical level, do something different, explore your edge with care.

- At the emotional level, reach out to someone new.
- At the mental level, read a book or an article outside your area of expertise.
- At the heart level, explore a new way to love.

Be One

Being one may not be easy in the digital age. We are distracted by an overload of information. We don't have time to process all of it. We go from one thing to the next, over stimulated and emotionally foggy. We have a plethora of activities, products, and services available that pull us in many directions and create a buzz at the mental and emotional levels. When we allow the mental or emotional parts of us to lead, it can cause separation. Depression, anxiety, and physical illness may manifest from this.

One is never enough from our mind's perspective. One is also not understood by our emotional self: we either go into fusion with another and loose our identity or we feel isolated. There is only one part of us that is able to connect to oneness: our heart center. It is a place without judgment, separation, or expectation.

Marta, one of Shari's clients, has spent many years searching for oneness. Her sense of self and identity were undeveloped. Marta explored numerous religions hoping to find a sense of wholeness. What became clear is that in order to feel complete she had to do some inner work and healing to strengthen her own sense of being. From there, choosing a spiritual path became easier for Marta.

Oneness begins from within. Your surroundings don't have to dictate your state of being. Have you ever felt miserable on a beautiful beach? How does a monk meditate when sirens are going off? Can you feel one when you don't have physical comfort? When you decide to pay attention to your inner experience, regardless of the circumstances, you open the door to oneness.

Being one does not mean that we must be like everyone else, agreeing with their point of view, or having the same habits. Being one requires the practice of self-love; this process entails embracing all our different parts. When we are aware of our complexity, we are one.

When you experience oneness from within, you will feel connected to everything and everyone. Ask yourself and make the necessary adjustments: Am I creating oneness or separation? Am I splitting myself, or am I bringing myself together?

No matter how many opportunities, you must not fragment yourself; remember that your true nature is to be one.

THE PRACTICE:

MEDITATION: OM MEDITATION

Om is a mantra found in Hinduism, (written AUM plus the silent syllable) Tibetan, and Buddhist tradition. It brings union between the mind, body, and spirit, and vibrates at the frequency of 432 Hz, which is said to be the natural frequency of the universe, the gateway to healing and wholeness.

- Sit in a comfortable position and close your eyes.
- Take a couple of breaths to center.
- Breathe in and on your long exhale chant or say OM.
- Continue for three minutes.

JOURNALING

- What gives you a feeling of oneness at the physical level?
- What gives you a feeling of oneness at the emotional level?
- What gives you a feeling of oneness at the mental level?
- What gives you a feeling of oneness at the heart level?

TAKE ACTION

- Identify an area in your life that causes separation within you. Decide what needs to change to create oneness. For example: If you are feeling incomplete or unheard after a conversation, the action would be to reach out and communicate your experience. Or, if your home, office or car is messy, and you feel scattered and agitated about it, the action would be to clear and clean the space.

BE PATIENT

We live in a world that does not promote patience. Speed is a selling point: fast food, fast check out, fast delivery, you name it. Being patient may feel like being in slow motion and not in control of desired outcomes. In brief, it feels like a punishment.

Yet, patience has nothing to do with waiting, stopping our flow, or hoping we will finally get what we want. It has to do with surrendering, being flexible, and being creative.

Often, we perceive patience as standing still, holding our breath, and being tense. Patience does not call on the performer within (How long can I wait?), it calls on the heart within (How can I embrace it?).

Patience is tested during challenging times. We may have experienced a significant loss, endured a long illness, or faced an unexpected obstacle and be tempted to escape. As we become frustrated, we may fall into a vicious cycle where we become impatient with our impatience. When patience is driven by our mind, we do not learn, and we do not grow.

The heart is the only part of us that can bring the quality of patience; it focuses on what is now, instead of what is next. The heart has a unique sense of time. Time becomes space, and the notion of slow or fast is not relevant.

There are two key components when cultivating patience. The first one is to let go and remain calm. The second one is to take advantage of the space given to you and to be grateful for it. This reframe allows constriction to unfold into expansion.

Next time you must wait, pause, step back, and assess the situation you are in. You may gain new insight that will help you along the way.

THE PRACTICE

MEDITATION: ONE-MINUTE BREATH

The purpose of this meditation is to cultivate calm and serenity while releasing anxiety. It requires focus, which in turn calls on your inner stability and patience.

- The pattern of this breath is to inhale through the nose slowly for 20 seconds, pause and hold the breath in for 20 seconds and exhale slowly through the nose for 20 seconds. Use this pattern, but change the duration of the inhale, pause and exhale to be able to do it for three minutes. You may start with 5 seconds. Work your way up.

JOURNALING

- Recall a situation where your patience was limited. Notice what happened in your body; notice your thoughts and emotions. What could you have done differently?

TAKE ACTION

- Reach out to someone you interact with regularly and ask for feedback regarding what they have noticed about your patience.

BE PLAYFUL

Playfulness is not a temporary activity reserved for our childhood; it is a quality that needs to be in our lives from the time of birth until our death.

In order to stay relaxed and not take things too seriously, our discipline should be to bring the spirit of playfulness. Our challenges are often met with defense mechanisms, and these prevent us from thinking outside the box and being resilient.

Playfulness rejects drama or victimhood. We don't fixate or go into flight or freeze mode. It provides a pathway to let go.

Catherine, a friend of Tejpal, was diagnosed in 2006 with LAM, or Lymphangioleiomyomatosis. It is a rare and deadly lung disease that has caused hundreds of small cysts to form in her lung tissues.

She was given five to ten years to live. Today her condition is stable, and she can live fully. Among the many healing practices she has tried, playfulness and laughter are certainly important ones. Catherine believes in the therapeutic power of humor. She has written humorist books, she teaches groups to help others reconnect to the power of laughter, and she uplifts so many with her spirit of playfulness.

Humor is an expression of playfulness. The practice of laughter in mind, body, spirit traditions is ancient. It became popular in the US at the end of the 20th century. The benefits are endless. Laughter increases the intake of oxygen, releases tension, improves our immune system, relieves pain, and uplifts our mood. Some people have asked for laughter and humor on their deathbed, to help relieve anxiety and fear. Budai, the Zen Buddhist Monk from the 10th century (well-known as the Laughing Buddha), is a good reminder that one can choose to be playful no matter what, even within the quiet and rigorous lifestyle of a monk.

Humor or playfulness does not take away the severity of an event, or the pain one endures. Grieving and mourning are essential to any healing process, while playfulness lightens a situation and may lead to transformations.

Being playful is being present and in the moment, not attached to an outcome. When being playful, it becomes easier to appreciate beauty and practice gratitude. Playfulness helps us soften the lens through which we see our lives. We are reminded that we are not in control and that the spirit of playfulness can be energizing and rejuvenating.

Instead of looking at life as a stern test, approach it as a constant adventure. Choose playfulness in your life; it will be great medicine for your spirit and your attitude.

THE PRACTICE
MEDITATION: LAUGHTER YOGA

The purpose of this meditation is to lower the level of the stress hormone cortisol and lower one's blood pressure. It helps to dedramatize any challenging situations and accept what life may bring.

- Stand and move your body freely.
- Clap your hands and synchronize the words "HO HO HA HA" for 30 seconds.
- Engage your belly and begin to laugh. At first, it may seem fake; stay with it for two minutes.

JOURNALING

- Remember a time when you took things too seriously: write about it. Imagine the same situation with a playful spirit. Journal about what you discover.

TAKE ACTION

- Pick a chore and bring a spirit of playfulness to this chore. For example: While washing dishes sing a silly song, while vacuuming dance with the vacuum cleaner.

BE QUIET

As a kid, if someone told you to be quiet it felt like a punishment: you had to stop. Whatever you were thinking, doing, or saying, you had to stop your momentum, hold your breath, and be in freeze mode.

We all have unique relationships with noise and quietness. For some, being quiet means boredom or no life force. For others, it creates anxiety or agitation. Noise then becomes the answer to relaxation. Having the television on as a background noise may seem the only way to fall asleep.

Quietness is not a quality that is usually valued. We are in constant mental chatter. Our mind likes to fill in any blank space with our neurosis. In meditation, you may have heard the instruction to quiet the mind. This may not be what you think it is. You may believe that if you are a good meditator, then you are able to have no thoughts, and that your mind is a blank canvas. Yet, as soon as you tune in, you realize how loud your mind is. The art of quieting the mind is to simply notice the movement of your thoughts, without emotional charge in a kind, loving way.

Quiet comes from within. It is the key to self-discovery. Being quiet is not about being absent; we can still have a quiet, yet powerful, presence. We are able to share our feelings, thoughts, and truth, yet, there is enough space for everyone to be. Developing and practicing a quiet presence teaches us to listen and have more respect. When we choose to be quiet, we become more neutral, which does not mean dull or uninterested. Our listening, our curiosity, and our understanding hold a wider spectrum. In a relationship, being quiet can be very comforting and peaceful. When we choose to be quiet, we choose not to be in control of the situation or someone else.

Nurture quietness in your life, so you can deepen your connections with everything and gain inner peace.

THE PRACTICE

MEDITATION: SOUND MEDITATION

The purpose of this meditation is to develop the art of being quiet by practicing curiosity and tuning in to a particular sense.

- Choose a location, inside or outside, and sit comfortably.
- Close your eyes and take a centering breath.
- For the next three minutes, notice all sounds: from your stomach growling, to the refrigerator, to the air conditioning, to the wind, the birds, etc.

JOURNALING

- Decide to journal about any random thoughts you may have every day for a week. Don't filter anything. Jump from one thing to another and notice your inner noise. Do it for five minutes every day.

TAKE ACTION

- Choose to create a quiet time and space in your life. For example: eat in silence, take a walk, take a break from all electronic devices, etc.

Be Ready

Being ready is often associated with two factors, time management and performance. For example: you are ready for a meeting, a phone call, or a conversation. If you have kids, you want them ready for bed, for school, for practice, etc. Since the notion of time is unique in different cultures, being ready can be the cause of misunderstandings between individuals and communities.

We are not interested in helping you enhance your ability to accomplish more; we are committed to helping you be more vibrant. If being ready is about anticipating everything that could happen, chances are you will be extremely busy all day long. This form of readiness creates on-going tension and prevents you from adapting and staying present, as you spend more time in the future, forecasting every step along the way.

Many things that happen to you, good or bad, are unpredictable. Most of us have said, "I was not ready for this," at some point. Guess what, when you are ready, it is too late. Readiness is trusting the intelligence of the heart and believing everything will be okay. Being ready is embracing losing or winning; it is being comfortable with the unknown.

Paul has been invited to go camping at a yoga retreat. Paul is forty, and even though he was initially enthusiastic, when the event drew closer, he became agitated, teary, and frustrated with himself. Paul had to face too many unknowns; he had never camped and was new to this yoga practice. He was afraid of being a burden. When he realized he was creating his own misery, he surrendered and ended up having a wonderful experience.

Some of you have been at a crossroads for way too long, waiting for the right time to make a decision. If you are looking for an insurance policy for every move you make, then you will become stuck. Being ready is not a concept based on your organizational skills; it is an exercise in faith and trust.

When we understand that life is not a performance and that being ready has nothing to do with avoiding catastrophes or failing, then we can breathe, and we don't have to live in fear. When we realize that being ready does not mean being on alert, ready to go, then we don't have to be constantly preoccupied, and we can relax at a deeper level.

The spirit of readiness is the spirit of no "BS" and no excuses for your behaviors or what is happening to you. It is the spirit of surrendering and accepting changes, it is the spirit of saying yes to life with all its beauty and challenges. *"Ready or not, here life comes!"*

THE PRACTICE

MEDITATION: EXPANDING BREATH

The purpose of this meditation is to help you relax, develop a spirit of flexibility, and trust what comes to you.

- Lie down in a quiet space.
- Allow your body to be supported by the floor, a bed, or the earth.
- Take a couple of breaths to release and settle.

- Put one hand on your lower belly and the other hand at the center of your chest.
- As you inhale, fill the belly with breath and continue to fill all the way up.
- As you exhale, preferably through the nose, release from the chest into the belly.
- As you continue this cycle, feel that you are riding the waves.
- Keep this image, spirit and momentum for the next three minutes.

JOURNALING

- Make a list of all the things you have thought of doing but never did. For example: taking an art class, studying archeology, or engaging in a volunteer activity. Reflect on what stopped you from doing these things.

TAKE ACTION

- Think about something you wanted to do, postponed, or avoided. Take a healthy risk and do it now.

BE REBELLIOUS

D on't try to fit in, you belong. Don't try to follow trends; they never last. Be rebellious. Don't say yes or follow authority just because. Pause, assess, question, and decide.

Being rebellious reminds you that your uniqueness matters. When who you are on the outside matches who you are on the inside, you are centered. Being rebellious is a way to check in and honor your true self, no matter what.

Perhaps you married someone from a different religion, tradition, race, or social milieu. Perhaps you chose not to take over the family business that has been in the family for generations. Being rebellious is listening to the fire within and taking action aligned with your true self.

Rebellion does not have to be about destruction or going against authority. It can be about being courageous enough to stay true to you, despite any expectations placed upon you.

Being rebellious is not about being eccentric and attracting attention; it is not about being special from the place of the ego. It is about being you, without worrying about what others think. It is about making choices and accepting that not everyone will understand you.

Alice, who is eighty-nine and lives in a retirement community, loves taking painting classes. Every time she has company, her company asks which grandchild painted the lovely art adorning her walls. With pride, she says, "I did it."

For centuries, religions and countries have condemned rebellion and threatened non-followers. A healthy culture respects diversity. If you want to learn something, question everything; be rebellious. When you do not tip-toe through life and you accept who you are, chances are you will be more alive.

Rebellion encourages radical change from within and the breaking of old patterns so that shift happens. Don't try to fit in.

THE PRACTICE

MEDITATION: LION BREATH

The purpose of this meditation is to clear toxins and balance your throat chakra. It may help you find your voice.

- Choose a position that feels right to you. Examples: easy pose, standing up, sitting on your heels, etc.
- Take a couple of centering breaths.
- Take a deep breath in and on the exhale open your mouth wide, stick out your tongue and roar like a lion.
- Continue for a minute.
- Close with a couple of centering breaths.

JOURNALING

- Journal about your own rebellion. What form did or does your rebellion take when you do so? Do you allow yourself to be rebellious? Does your rebellion serve you to grow, or is it a form of resistance?

TAKE ACTION

- Choose an art form and express the essence of rebellion.

BE SACRED

Being sacred is not necessarily about your connection to specific religions or divinities; it is an experience from within.

Being sacred is a lifestyle. You don't need to wait for special lifecycle events to occur to be reminded of the sacred; it is an ongoing practice beyond birth, death, or marriage. You can bring grace and therefore, sacredness, to your everyday.

Being sacred is not about being grandiose or extravagant; it is not about being special or mysterious. It is about honoring and respecting who we are, from moment to moment. Everything we do and experience can be sacred: walking in a forest, listening or playing music, preparing or sharing a meal. The expressions of sacredness are endless.

Sacredness blends well with simplicity; it also teaches us to open and quiet our emotions and our mind. From there, you realize that preciousness is everywhere: from a rain drop to a rainbow, from a rock to a mountain, from a child's drawing to a masterpiece.

When being sacred becomes the foundation of your lifestyle, you will experience pain differently. Instead of grabbing and clinging to the discomfort, you can welcome every experience as a gift.

For example, Sally is a researcher in the field of medicine and has been working at a lab for many years. Lately, the pressure of productivity has been such that she decided to quit. Unable to find someone to replace her, the company asked her to stay. They agreed to a two day per week contract. As she started to step aside, she realized that the work she was involved in was not fulfilling. Without the constant pressure, Sally would have stayed without questioning her lack of fulfillment. Now she is exploring speaking and teaching opportunities, as well as other research projects she is passionate about.

Being sacred does not guarantee happiness, or even look for it. Its purpose is one of depth and meaning. If you commit to the sacred, you are taking the journey of devotion and compassion, which leads to an open heart. It invites us to live in a new paradigm beyond the polarities of the mind, such as right and wrong or good and bad.

Depending on your country and religion, what is considered sacred varies. In some parts of India, cows are sacred. For many Native Americans, the land is sacred. Many yoga classes end with the sacred mantra, "Namaste," which means, "The divine in me bows to the divine in you."

Instead of creating division as to what you think should be sacred or not, consider that everything is, and stay curious. The sacred does not need to have a golden fence around it and be available to only a few. The sacred is who you are, if you take the time to go within.

THE PRACTICE

MEDITATION: BOWING MEDITATION

The purpose of this meditation is to help you develop some key qualities of the heart: humility, respect, listening, gratefulness, and acceptance.

- Practice a bowing meditation. Depending on your tradition and what your body allows, do this on your knees, on a chair, or standing up.
- Do this eleven times.

JOURNALING

- What do you consider sacred in your life? How do you relate to the sacred? What does the sacred bring to you? How could you bring more sacred into your life?

TAKE ACTION

- Identify an area of your life where you want more grace, respect, devotion, and kindness.
- Implement this change.

BE SINGLE

Don't worry, you don't have to break up or get divorced if you are in a relationship!

Being single is not just about your relationship status. It is much more about you and your inner self. Pause, remember who you are, respect your singularity, and reconnect to self.

In America, there is still a bias that suggests happiness and romantic relationships are linked; without one, we cannot have the other. The thought process is often one of, if you have not been in a relationship for a long time, there is definitively something wrong with you. There must be a reason. You are not sexy or smart, you are emotionally unbalanced and maybe even broken, you are defective and unworthy of love. Movies, TV shows, and advertising do not often depict well-adjusted single characters. We still believe the old fairy tale that says being single is a stigma. Couples rarely invite single friends unless they want to "fix them up." As children, we most likely did not envision being single as an adult. The dating service business is booming and in 2018 reached 2.5 billion dollars. Still, the number of single adults over eighteen years old is growing and comprised 45% of the population in 2017.

Can we embrace a new way of looking at being single? Can we embrace the idea that being single is not a default, but a choice? Can we embrace the idea that single people don't need to be fixed or fixed up?

Relationships can be wonderful, yet they aren't the answer to being happy. If you respect your uniqueness and give yourself permission to have experiences without a partner, you may feel refreshed. Just because you are with someone, does not mean you are really with them. You may go along without pausing, thinking, and feeling, and eventually fall asleep. When you allow yourself to be single in a relationship, you connect with who you truly are, gain insight, and deepen your intimacy.

Being single does not mean being lonely. Feeling isolated can occur whether you are married or single, surrounded by many, or on your own. Being single invites you to question what you really want and who you are; it is a growth opportunity.

If you are looking for others to distract you or fill your void, then being single is a struggle. You may fall into co-dependent relationships and open the door to a world of swirling emotions that prevents personal growth. The spirit of being single invites you to have your own voice and a strong sense of self.

THE PRACTICE

MEDITATION: ONE BREATH

The purpose of this meditation is to embrace what is and let go. It will teach you to stay away from perfection (there is no do-over) and accept what is.

- The practice of this meditation consists of one single breath.
- Sit in a comfortable position. Lengthen your spine and draw your shoulders down your

back. Soften your face and your jaw. Close your eyes.

- Take one long breath in and out.
- Notice the quality of your experience.

JOURNALING

- Whether or not you are in a committed relationship, what does being single mean to you? Explore your own preconceived notions and give yourself permission to look at it differently. What are the benefits of being single? How can you enjoy these benefits whether or not you are in a relationship?

TAKE ACTION

- Explore activities on your own and notice your experience. For example: go to a movie, concert, theater, or exhibit on your own. Take a weekend by yourself.

BE SLOW

"Slow down!" How many times have you heard or given this advice to someone else? You know the benefits of slowing down, but do you know the benefits of being slow?

Don't slow down because you are going too fast. Don't slow down because you are recovering from an illness or an injury or a major achievement. Do slow down when you think you don't need to.

The world we live in makes us think that going fast is the ticket. One opinion after another is sent into this big social media vortex of constant reactivity. A few words, a picture, and bang! You may be tempted to keep up with the pace of social media, and if you do, it will consume you.

When you refer to someone as slow, it means that the person has some deficiencies: brilliance equals fast. We love to juggle a million thoughts at once and accomplish a lot in a short amount of time.

For some, going fast is exhilarating and liberating; you feel alive and energized. But the truth is, you are running on adrenaline and eventually will crash. We are all familiar with the fable, *The Tortoise and the Hare;* slow and steady wins the race. Yet, deep inside you still believe that being slow creates sluggishness, lethargy, and a lack of motivation.

Our mind and emotions are constantly reactive. When we desire something, we want it now; when we are in pain, we want to be rid of it as soon as possible. Our mind and emotions feed each other and create this fast momentum that generates chaos and confusion. Everything is seen as urgent.

When you choose to be slow, even if your mind or body could go fast, you expand your consciousness. You are more aware of your feelings, surroundings, and senses. When being slow is a choice, you open your heart and you connect to everything on a deeper level. When you choose a slow pace, the path is it. You are not obsessed with the outcomes and not willing to make compromises or shortcuts to achieve something.

Our breath is often too fast and too shallow. A lack of oxygen in the blood generates different kinds of physical illnesses. Practicing slow, conscious breathing will help us to be mindful, instead of on alert.

Be slow, even if it is unpleasant at first; be slow, and you will find peace.

THE PRACTICE

MEDITATION: SLOWING DOWN

The purpose of this meditation is to enhance your focus and concentration; it is more challenging to stay present as you slow down.

- Practice this breath first in a quiet place; eventually, you can do it anywhere.
- Soften your gaze or close your eyes.
- Take a couple of breaths to center.
- Consciously slow down your inhale and exhale.

- Notice if your body and mind tend to resist, or if you allow a slower breath to guide you.
- Continue to practice slowing down your inhale and exhale for three minutes.

JOURNALING

- Journal about your resistance to slowing down or being slow.

TAKE ACTION

- Choose one activity, routine, or part of your day and approach it slowly.
- Examples could be a meal, commute to work, etc.

BE SMALL

Small is generally not valued in traditional American culture; big is viewed as better. For a long time, we have promoted big cars, big houses, the Big Mac; you name it. Big is perceived as a sign of success. In the economic world we live in, big always sneaks in with mega merger deals between corporations.

What if you choose to be small and go against the mainstream? Would you be able to notice with more accuracy what is going on around you? Would you listen differently? Would you express yourself differently? Would you let go of the need to be at the center? When you choose to be small, you practice humility.

It takes a good level of self-esteem to be small. When you are comfortable with who you are, you don't have to be big and you don't need attention.

Being small gives you the opportunity to be respectful of others and the environment.

When we realize happiness has nothing to do with "big", and we realize big always looks for bigger, then you know it is time to explore a new paradigm. When we eat a small meal, we often take more time to appreciate and savor each bite. We may even discover new flavors and texture.

If one lives or works in a small space, one learns to be deliberate about what one truly needs and how to be organized. We approach the space differently as we clarify what is important. We can then eliminate or dismiss any clutter.

The practice of being small teaches you how to say goodbye. There is no need to accumulate, guard, and over protect. There is no need to have more than what you need. Having a lot, or more than you need, does not necessarily provide a sense of feeling good or a sense of safety. When you choose to be small, you are less distracted and more aware of what is truly important to you. When practicing being small, you don't compare yourself to others, and you start paying attention to your needs. Doing so makes it much easier to set boundaries.

Being small does not require restricting yourself or holding back, but it does teach you the art of being present and discreet. It invites you to be concise in your communication. It supports you in carefully choosing your focus and actions. It invites you to be sensitive to everything, and it helps you adapt to various situations.

If you want to be aware, be small.

THE PRACTICE

MEDITATION: CHILD POSE

The purpose of this meditation is to go within while releasing tension. A few benefits of this practice are to calm your mind, enhance your digestion, and help you rest.

- Begin on your hands and knees. Take a couple of breaths.
- Let your big toes touch and spread your knees.
- Slowly let your hips move towards your heels as your chest lowers towards the ground.

- Arm Variation:
  - Arms stretched out in front of you, palms facing down on the floor.
  - Make a pillow with your hands to relax your forehead on.
  - Bring your arms down by your side, palms facing up.
- Soften and steady your breath for three minutes.

JOURNALING

- Write about an area that is difficult for you to find moderation within. Examples range from behaviors to possessions. Such as, when I go out to dinner, I find it difficult to limit my food and alcohol intake, or, I have ten white t-shirts. Identify and explore the attachments, rational, and the purpose it serves.

TAKE ACTION

- Practice being small. Choose one of the following:
  - Buy a smaller purse or backpack.
  - Have small meals for a day.
  - Shop small at the grocery store (30% of what we buy is wasted).

BE SOFT

Typically, being soft is not perceived as a great characteristic. It means you are a nice person with perhaps a lack of character and an inability to confront and/or address difficult situations. In a few words, being soft is often seen as a weakness.

Being soft does not mean being absent, weak, fearful, or fragile. Being soft prevents impulsivity. Our suffering often lies within our reactivity. Without extreme highs or lows, we gain clarity and peace. The discipline of being soft is found in moderation.

Practicing softness is about noticing and not dulling. If you choose to soften your gaze, your voice, or your touch, you become more aware. Softening awakens the witness within. As you soften, resistance softens. Barriers and obstacles are toned down, and there is a new horizon of possibilities and creativity. Softening promotes acceptance and collaboration.

There is a level of comfort that allows different points of view to be expressed. There is a level of tolerance and fluidity. It is easier to be heard when you are soft. It also encourages others to soften and brings an attitude of relaxation, as well as creating serenity.

Being soft enhances the quality of your life by allowing you to release unnecessary tension. It allows you to be quiet and still. There is no need to create unnecessary waves. Being soft reminds us of our impermanence; nothing is forever.

Softness brings a level of stability and peace. The opposite of softness is rigidity. Rigidity leads to attachment, irritability, agitation, and stress. Softness helps you realize there is no need to fight, push, or force, and that your focus is to be with what is. It takes attention and intention to be soft. Softness is the expression of surrender, and surrendering is your path to happiness.

Rigidity conquers, while softness invites. Rigidity creates division, while softness creates connection. Which do you choose?

THE PRACTICE

MEDITATION: SQUEEZE AND RELEASE

The purpose of this meditation is to help release tension and create deep relaxation. This practice entails squeezing on the inhale and releasing on the exhale.

- Lie down in a quiet and comfortable place.
- Take a couple of breaths.
- Begin the practice at your toes: squeeze on the inhale and release on the exhale.
- Repeat two more times.
- Continue moving up the body focusing on your feet, ankles, calves, knees, thighs, bottom, belly, etc.
- After you complete this process, squeeze your entire body on the inhale and release on the exhale.

JOURNALING

- What are the ways and areas you would like to soften?

TAKE ACTION

- Choose an area you are going to soften for the entire day. It could be your driving style, your communication, your thoughts, etc.

BE SURPRISED

When was the last time you were surprised? Pause for a moment; what thoughts arise within you? Are you thinking of a joyful surprise or a painful one? Perhaps you have vivid memories of unpleasant surprises: a loved one is injured, your car breaks down, a friend cancels a dinner, etc. Can you also recall pleasant surprises?

The more you allow surprises in your life, the more adaptable and livelier you become. This principle applies in many ways: athletes who always train the same way will not make a lot of progress. It is a change of patterns that create strong and healthy bodies.

Being surprised calls on your sensitivity, your awareness, and your curiosity. By paying attention to your surroundings, you may find yourself surprised by the shape of a cloud, a butterfly, the shadow of a tree, or the smell of a candle.

Being surprised is an attitude of openness and receptivity. Being surprised allows your heart to guide instead of your mind so that you can be engaged in every moment. You can listen to someone with the intent of being surprised, and most likely you will be. Or you can show up blasé, and that will be your experience. Boredom happens when you shut down and close your heart. A closed heart does not allow for anything new, or for surprises.

Our preconceived ideas and fears may also prevent us from allowing surprises into our lives. Our wounded self may shut the door to unexpected situations. Our emotional baggage can get in the way.

You may not like surprises because you are afraid of losing control. Embrace your sensitivity and accept your raw vulnerability. Allow your spontaneity to be part of your life and take the risk to be messy with your emotions. Each time you want to control something, your life force goes away. Controlling is resisting life. You may have forgotten how to be surprised because you are not present: your routine takes over and you disappear into your roles and duties.

If you are not able to be open and receive the myriad of events around you, your life is literally monotone. If you allow yourself to hold onto a beginner's mind, then everything will be new again. Any surprise is a life test. Through unpredictable situations, you grow and learn more about yourself.

Be surprised, and surprise others as well. Don't be predictable; allow yourself to feel vibrant again.

THE PRACTICE

MEDITATION: MIRROR MEDITATION

The purpose of this meditation is to help you shift from your automatic way of looking at yourself and open to new possibilities.

- Sit in a comfortable position in front of a mirror and look at yourself.
- Are you able to be surprised when you look at yourself or do you get fixated on the same aspects of your physical body?
- What will it take for you to be surprised by yourself?
- Continue for three minutes.

JOURNALING

- Assess your last 24 hours and journal about any surprises you experienced.

TAKE ACTION

- What can you do to bring the spirit of surprise into your life? For example, surprise a coworker by bringing them a special treat, surprise a loved one with flowers or a ticket to a performance, surprise yourself by showing up at a gathering. Be open and ready to be surprised.

BE UNCERTAIN

Our mind feels threatened when uncertainty occurs, and it creates a deep level of insecurity within us. If we could connect to our physical experience, deep enough to relax into who we are, we would realize that uncertainty is simply being. If we stay stuck in our finite social identity, we may use our will and positive thinking to believe that uncertainty is great, but within us, there will be tension and fear.

Many cultures don't know how to welcome uncertainty. Economic and societal models are based on predictability. We are in a constant search for answers as opposed to sitting with the unknown.

If you connect deeply within yourself, uncertainty becomes awareness and presence, moment to moment. We must train ourselves on how to welcome uncertainty. If we listen to the yogis, we have three minds: the negative, the positive, and the neutral. Each of the three minds is necessary for our well-being. The negative mind is the fastest and the first one to kick in; it helps us stay safe and be aware of simple dangers. The positive mind is the second one to be activated; it allows us to be open to possibilities. The third mind is the neutral one. This neutrality can only occur when we have explored the positive and negative aspects of every situation. The neutral mind allows us to see things for what they are (nothing more or less), without attachment and bias. The neutral mind embraces uncertainty, which requires practice to activate. Each of us has a unique balance of these three minds and can change the pattern and the balance.

Without any connection to self, uncertainty is something we try to avoid at all costs, as one may become addicted, depressed, worried, and/or withdrawn. Your linear mind is attached to knowing and leads you to believe that not knowing is dangerous. You cannot satisfy your mind by giving the mind what it asks for. You must shift and change the model from which you live. To do this, one must use more of the physical body and heart as the main organs of perception. When you integrate the different parts of your being, you can embrace the constant chaos of life.

When uncertainty is the way to be, we are then open and connected to everything else. When uncertainty becomes a threat, we end up being more disconnected. From the rational mind, uncertainty separates us; from the heart, uncertainty unites us. Instead of pushing uncertainty away, choose to embrace it and experience the wholeness within.

THE PRACTICE

MEDITATION: WALKING MEDITATION

The purpose of this meditation is to help you slow down, while also encouraging focus and concentration.

- When you walk, just walk. There is nowhere to go, no number of steps to count, no specific calories to burn. Just walk. Give yourself enough time afterwards to prevent having to rush into the next activity.
- This meditation can be done indoors or out.
- Begin by standing and taking a few breaths to ground and center.

- Be intentional and deliberate about each step.
- As you walk, connect with your breath and all your senses.
- Allow ten minutes.

JOURNALING: THE THREE MINDS

- Pick a situation in your life in which you want to gain clarity.
- Take a couple of minutes and write about how you relate to the situation from the perspective of your negative mind.
- Then take another couple of minutes and write how you relate to the situation from the perspective of the positive mind.
- Then take another couple of minutes and write how you relate to the situation from the perspective of the neutral mind.
- Pause and reflect on the different aspects.

TAKE ACTION

- Choose an area of personal change. This could be a new way of eating, exercising, socializing, or learning.
- Embrace not knowing the outcomes and try something different.

BE UNCOMFORTABLE

Comfort is something we all seek. The notion of being comfortable is well promoted in our society and considered a good selling point if you are buying a bed, clothes, a car, shoes, or most anything. If comfort is a great value in our lives, we can't be attached to it and push discomfort away at any price. Life events may be challenging and unfamiliar. If we are clinging to any form of comfort, we will limit our ability to adapt and grow. Over the years, over-promoting comfort, happiness, or pleasure has created tremendous distortions. There is no tolerance for any amount of discomfort and tremendous impatience for any kind of pain. This may lead to over-medicating, gaming, and other addictive behaviors. When comfort is the only choice, resilience and the ability to overcome any adversity are lost.

If you want to stay centered and at peace, you need to stop running away from discomfort (or running toward pleasure). Running from discomfort prevents you from being able to see and feel what is present. It holds you in a false state of reality and never allows you to know your true self. Being uncomfortable teaches you to transcend pain and pleasure, thus allowing you to be true to yourself. It also allows you to see clearly when challenges occur.

Constantly promoting pleasure and comfort has contributed to the creation of addictive behaviors. For example, many will use food as a comfort to soothe their pain or when experiencing stress. It starts with a tremendous obsession of the mind that makes us believe there is only one way. When our mind gets frantic about one thing, there is no room for anything else, and our behavior becomes extremely reactive. As soon as we grasp for more comfort, we become intoxicated. Intoxication does not necessarily have to involve a substance, such as alcohol. We can be intoxicated with power or greed. As soon as we are intoxicated, we lose our intelligence and our ability to be present.

When you experience discomfort, we suggest you stay away from labeling, contracting, and wondering when the pain will go away. Nobody came to earth to suffer, yet nobody came to earth to run away from suffering. Every time you hit your limitations, you have the opportunity to unfold and open.

Mara, one of our clients, was fired from her job. She was in her mid-fifties and worried about her future. In her exit interview, she was confronted with her behavior: she missed work and did not follow through with her responsibilities. Mara knew that alcohol was a problem in her life and had not addressed the issue. By hitting a wall, she had an opportunity to look at her problem and find the right support to help her shift. She realized how harshly she judged herself and that the alcohol was a vehicle to soothe her on-going self-rejection.

The purpose of pain is to awaken the heart, not trigger the mind. It is not about overcoming pain; it is about recognizing and being willing to learn from it. By opening her heart, Mara can now change her behavior and heal from her pain.

Meditation is a great way to learn to be still with discomfort. Many people express difficulties when trying to learn to meditate and often give up, believing they are not good at it. The purpose of meditation is not to add pleasure or pain, but to develop a neutral mind that allows whatever arises. Consistency in a meditation practice paves the way for acceptance and humility, two beautiful qualities of the heart.

If you are able to stay still during pain, without hoping for pleasure to come, you are free. If instead of fighting against the pain you welcome it fully, you will shift and heal. When this happens, you will realize that pain and pleasure are not opposites, but simply sensations; you are now living beyond polarities.

Being uncomfortable does not always relate to pain and pleasure; our own fears and limitations can create great discomfort. To avoid discomfort we may prevent ourselves from taking risks and put our self-development on hold. Some may feel stuck and have pushed the pause button while others might operate on auto pilot by staying busy with their to-do list. For example, some people may stay in a relationship or job even though they know it is no longer serving them. Both are forms of avoidance.

Allow discomfort to be part of your experience and welcome it fully from the heart center. At the core of your pain or fear, you will grow, and you will learn.

THE PRACTICE

MEDITATION: TONGLEN

Tonglen is a meditation practice found in Tibetan Buddhism and used to awaken compassion. Through acknowledging our own and others' suffering, we open our hearts.

- Sit in a comfortable position. Lengthen your spine and draw your shoulders down your back. Soften your face and your jaw. Close your eyes.
- Connect to one part of you that is in pain, at a physical, emotional, mental, heart or spiritual level.
- Notice the quality of your pain.

- Imagine all the people with a similar experience and inhale their pain.
- Exhale; send relief.
- Repeat the process for three minutes.

JOURNALING

- Think of something that makes you uncomfortable. Is this new or old? What are the main emotions you are experiencing? What behaviors or strategies have you implemented? What did you learn about yourself?

TAKE ACTION

- Do something out of your comfort zone.
- What did you learn?

BE UNPREDICTABLE

Saying someone is unpredictable is usually not a compliment. It might mean you can't count on them; you must keep your distance to prevent being hurt or betrayed. That form of unpredictability is certainly not what we are looking for, as it is led by erratic emotions.

What if unpredictability was the seed of vibrant living? What if unpredictability was what we need to practice, as it requires being completely present moment to moment? What if unpredictability was a core value to keep you awake, not from a place of being guarded and on alert, but from a place of being conscious and curious?

When you choose unpredictability as part of your lifestyle, it encourages flexibility. You can change your priorities, adapt your schedule as you stay in tune with your inner experience and the different events in your life.

When you choose unpredictability, you don't fall into a routine that takes over who you are and causes you to become rigid or apathetic. Unpredictability allows you to experience and embrace every situation with grace; it is truly going with the flow. It also gives you an avenue for self-expression without limitations.

Being unpredictable is taking the risk to shift your pace, patterns, and experiences. You are not changing for the sake of changing, you are not changing because you are afraid of boredom; you are changing because you let everything unfold without control.

We all have experienced very predictable family celebrations: we know who will tell the same jokes, who worries about the same thing, who vents about the same event, etc. If you choose to be unpredictable and tap into your infinite self, your infinite silliness and sense of adventure, then you will be willing to go for a ride! You are still responsible, and you keep your word and commitments. Yet, you decide how to show up in a way that is authentic, fresh, and beyond any expectations.

Stay present and let go of your attachments to be this or have that so that your unpredictable self can flourish for the good of everyone and everything. Find comfort in unpredictability. If you want to be alive, be unpredictable.

THE PRACTICE

MEDITATION: EXPLORE YOUR BREATH PATTERNS

The purpose of this meditation is to help you embrace unpredictability and develop a new level of tolerance. By practicing a diversity of breath, you will be able to adapt to other areas of your life.

- Sit in a comfortable position. Lengthen your spine and draw your shoulders down your back. Soften your face and your jaw. Close your eyes.
- Inhale through the nose and exhale through the mouth; repeat this cycle five times. Pause and notice how you feel.
- Then inhale through the mouth and exhale through the nose; repeat this cycle five times. Pause and notice how you feel.

- Then inhale through the nose and exhale through the nose; repeat this cycle five times. Pause and notice how you feel.
- Finally, inhale through the mouth and exhale through the mouth; repeat this cycle four times. Pause and notice how you feel.

JOURNALING

- Journal about the things you can't control and what you may need to let go of.

TAKE ACTION

- Your lifestyle: Assess your routine and decide what you need to change. First, make a list of your daily routine, from waking up, to working out, to driving to work, etc. Then, identify domains where you would like to practice unpredictability.

BE USELESS

There are two values which are repeatedly rewarded: productivity and efficiency. In the seventies, everyone who worked in the corporate world had to take a time management workshop; accomplishing more was "the thing." We now face a different time period where doing more seems less appealing, but don't be fooled by it. Regardless of the era or the trend, we still get caught up in being productive.

We run all day long, managing a crisis or chasing a dream. If you call a friend, your first question most likely will be, "What are you up to?" or "What are you doing?" instead of, "How are you?" We are so wired with the doing that it becomes the most important thing. We can feel the buzz from going non-stop and yet, at the end of the day we wonder what happened. We can experience a false sense of purpose and a shallow feeling of recognition by constantly doing.

When this happens, as soon as we pause, we crash and "hit the wall." We eat, drink, smoke, or buy stuff because there is too much agitation inside of us. We have lost our ability to feel and listen; we have lost our serenity and clarity. Everything becomes reactive, and we don't really know what truly matters to us.

Every human being has a feminine and masculine polarity. Our masculine polarity focuses on achieving, and our feminine polarity focuses on our emotions and the flow of energy. If our identity leads into how much we have done, we are trapped in our masculine polarity. Being useless teaches us to balance our feminine and masculine polarity.

By banking on productivity, you might be missing out on meaningful opportunities.

To create meaning, start by practicing being useless. Let go of your productive self and reflect. Self-examination helps you to know what is important to you. The mind does not know how to be useless; it will pull you into a to-do list, into any kind of situation that will propel you into a "busy bee" paradigm.

Being useless invites you to go within and pay attention to your sensations. It puts the linear mind aside and provides the opportunity to embrace the day in a meditative way. You are allowing things to come your way. Your relationship with time changes and everything becomes more spacious.

Choose to go on a mind fast, a mind reset, and be useless.

THE PRACTICE
MEDITATION:
CANDLE GAZING MEDITATION

The purpose of this meditation is to attune the mind with the flame of a candle: wandering without a specific purpose, letting the thoughts come and go. It helps the mind to release thoughts and disconnect from any particular agenda.

- Sit in a comfortable position in a quiet place and light a candle.
- Gaze at the flame for three minutes

JOURNALING

- Journal about how being useful has served you. Then, identify ways you can practice being useless. For example, looking at a fireplace, watching kids playing outside, or reading a novel.

TAKE ACTION

- Take an hour and choose to be useless. What does it look like? Notice your resistance or anxiety in doing so.

BE WRONG

What's wrong with being wrong? We often will argue or blame and do anything to avoid being wrong. Being wrong does not have to be painful. When we choose to take responsibility for being wrong, it sets us free.

When we identify our whole self with being wrong, we experience shame and want to run away or hide. When we recognize that our actions or words are wrong and realize that our sense of self is not attacked, we can be curious about the root cause of our behavior.

Can we normalize being wrong? Can we acknowledge, without making up a story, that we are often wrong? Can a day go by without one saying the wrong thing, making the wrong turn, or ordering the wrong item on the menu? We are so afraid and so triggered that we will use many forms of defense mechanisms. We also react in various ways: we play small, don't take risks, and don't speak up.

Most businesses have a low tolerance when it comes to mistakes and lose sight of the bigger picture when mistakes happen. Time is spent on covering, justifying, and defending, instead of focusing on what needs to happen.

Athletes and performers make mistakes all the time. They are not afraid to analyze the process, because by doing so, they learn and improve their skills. Their drive for excellence opens their understanding, allowing them to assess what went wrong and make the necessary adjustments.

Successful discoveries and innovations are often the result of mistakes. Two good examples are the invention of penicillin and Post-It Notes. In both cases, someone inadvertently realized the item, previously considered useless, could be beneficial and offer health benefits (penicillin) or time saving (Post-It Notes) to many people.

Set your pride aside; give yourself the gift of experiencing humility. When being wrong is no longer an issue, you have less anxiety and insecurity. When being wrong is part of your being, you will find you are less often attached to what is right or wrong.

Be wrong; your failures are often your best lessons.

THE PRACTICE

MEDITATION: SEATED FORWARD BEND

This pose has many physical benefits, and it also calms the mind and reduces anxiety. Bending forward invites you to practice humility as you may not be able to perfect the pose.

- Begin seated with the legs straight in front of you.
- If you have a back issue, sit against a wall.
- Flex your feet and engage your legs. Ideally the back of the legs are pressing against the floor.
- Inhale; lift your arms and draw your shoulders down the back.
- Exhale; lead with your heart as you lengthen and lower your torso towards your legs. Your hands may rest on your legs, your shins, or your feet.

- Breathe and release into the pose for three minutes.

JOURNALING

- Reflect on a time when you struggled with being wrong. What was underneath it? What were your fears and defense mechanisms?

TAKE ACTION

- We give you three options:
- Take the risk of being wrong. For example, speak up in a situation you may normally withdraw from out of fear, or engage in an activity you may not be good at.
- Admit it when you realize you are wrong.
- Receive and respond with openness when someone calls you out on being wrong.

CONCLUSION

THE DISCIPLINE TO BE YOU

We have one wish for you
It is for you to be you.
And forgive us for being so demanding,
Forgive us for directing you or imposing on you
in any way.
We own our distortions of hope for you
And in that hope, we are not conditional.
There is no deadline, no one way ticket.

Yet, if you knock at our door
That is what we offer you…nothing else…
Be you, beyond your physical attachments,
Your roles, your look, your age, your belongings,
your relationships.
Be you, awake, and at peace with the constant
unfolding of who you truly are.

It takes discipline to be you.
It will take all of you and more to never betray
yourself from fear-
Of not having enough, being rejected, failing, or
whatever else your fear pulls you to do.
It takes lucidity to look at your shadow and
forgive yourself over and over.

It takes trust

And the courage to die over and over.
So you don't get attached to your fixed identity
or what you know.

This is the kind of discipline we are talking about,
The discipline of the heart.

If you realize that in the chaos of your life and
mind there is no other way
Then knock at our door.
And in the space between us, you will find You.

With much love,

Tejpal and Shari

Other Books by Tejpal (with Dr. Carrol McLaughlin)

Manifest Moment to Moment:
8 Principles to Create the Life You Truly
Desire (Hay House, Inc. 2014)

Made in the USA
San Bernardino, CA
26 June 2020